RELIGION
IN THE
SCHOOLS

A Reference Handbook

Other Titles in ABC-CLIO's
CONTEMPORARY
WORLD ISSUES
Series

Abortion, Second Edition, Marie Costa
Adoption, Barbara Moe
AIDS Crisis in America, Second Edition, Eric K. Lerner and Mary Ellen Hombs
Campaign and Election Reform, Glenn H. Utter and Ruth Ann Strickland
Children's Rights, Beverly C. Edmonds and William R. Fernekes
Cults, James R. Lewis
Feminism, Judith Harlan
Gangs, Karen L. Kinnear
Intellectual Freedom, John B. Harer
Public Schooling in America, Richard D. Van Scotter
The Religious Right, Glenn H. Utter and John W. Storey
School Violence, Deborah L. Kopka

Books in the Contemporary World Issues series address vital issues in today's society such as terrorism, sexual harassment, homelessness, AIDS, gambling, animal rights, and air pollution. Written by professional writers, scholars, and nonacademic experts, these books are authoritative, clearly written, up-to-date, and objective. They provide a good starting point for research by high school and college students, scholars, and general readers, as well as by legislators, businesspeople, activists, and others.

Each book, carefully organized and easy to use, contains an overview of the subject; a detailed chronology; biographical sketches; facts and data and/or documents and other primary-source material; a directory of organizations and agencies; annotated lists of print and nonprint resources; a glossary; and an index.

Readers of books in the Contemporary World Issues series will find the information they need in order to better understand the social, political, environmental, and economic issues facing the world today.

RELIGION
IN THE
SCHOOLS

A Reference Handbook

James John Jurinski

**CONTEMPORARY
WORLD ISSUES**

ABC-CLIO

Santa Barbara, California
Denver, Colorado
Oxford, England

Library of Congress Cataloging-in-Publication Data

Jurinski, James.
    Religion in the schools : a reference handbook / James John
Jurinski.
        p. cm.—(Contemporary world issues)
    Includes bibliographical references (p.) and index.
    ISBN 0–87436–868–5
    1. Religion in the public schools—United States—Handbooks,
Manuals, etc. 2. Religion in the public schools—Law and
legislation—United States—Handbooks, manuals, etc. 3. Religious
education—United States—Handbooks, manuals, etc. 4. Church
schools—United States—Handbooks, manuals, etc. I. Title.
II. Series.
LC111.J87   1998
379.2'8'0973—dc21   98–20905
                                                                                      CIP

04 03 02 01 00 99 98 10 9 8 7 6 5 4 3 2 1

ABC-CLIO, Inc.
130 Cremona Drive, P.O. Box 1911
Santa Barbara, California 93116–1911

This book is printed on acid-free paper ∞ .

Manufactured in the United States of America

Contents

Preface

Religion in the schools is one of the most contentious issues facing the United States, an issue that will no doubt continue to be important well into the next century. America was founded on the concept of religious freedom. Indeed, many of the earliest colonists came to America to practice their religion, and freedom of religion is guaranteed by the First Amendment to the U.S. Constitution, which provides that the government shall not establish a religion or inhibit the free exercise of religion. Americans enjoy almost unlimited opportunities to practice the religion of their choice. In fact, no other country has such diversity of religion.

Although most Americans agree that the constitutional guarantee of freedom of religion is one of our most treasured protections, there is little agreement about how this freedom should be expressed in the public schools. On one side are the absolutists, who argue that the Constitution mandates a "wall of separation" between church and state. Proponents of this view believe that religion is a personal and family matter and should be kept out of the schools. These absolutists argue that a schoolteacher posting a copy of the Ten Commandments in the classroom promotes Christianity and Judaism in an impermissible way. On the other side of the issue are accommodationists, who believe that schools should not be godless zones. They believe that religious individuals should be free to express their religion. Further, they often argue that if the majority desire to have a prayer or Bible reading in the classroom, then students of other religions could remain silent or be excluded from the classroom. Some proponents of this view also argue that the biblical account of Adam and Eve should be taught along with the theory of evolution in biology classes. Americans have strong views about religion and also about the content of school curriculums. When these two issues coincide passions can be ignited, and the heterogeneity of American religious practice can cause problems for the public school system.

Importance of Law

Many of the controversies surrounding religion in the schools have found their way to the courtroom, and laws and court decisions have come to shape the patterns of the school day. The law will decide if a minister can say a prayer at the high school graduation. The law will decide if a nativity scene can be placed in front of the elementary school at Christmastime.

In the United States, the ultimate arbiter of the law is the Supreme Court, and over the years the Court has been at the center of many of these controversies. Congress is also an important player through its lawmaking power, and understanding the relationship of Congress and the Court will help illuminate how the law evolves in this area.

The court cases excerpted in Chapter 4 of this book are important not only because they define the contours of the law on issues involving religion in the schools, but also because they illustrate how the legal system deals with real disputes that need to be reconciled. The cases illustrate that while it is easy to devise rules, it can be far harder to apply those rules to specific real-life situations. This chapter contains not only majority court opinions, but also dissenting opinions showing that Supreme Court justices—like other Americans—do not always agree on how these issues should be resolved. In some cases the logic in one of the Court's dissenting opinions later becomes the logic that the Court uses in another case.

Current Issues

I will examine several aspects of religion in the schools. Although some disputes defy easy categorization, there are six major areas of controversy.

School Prayer and Other In-school Religious Activities

Forty years ago it was common for American schoolchildren to start the school day by reciting the Lord's Prayer or by reading a passage from the Bible. After these practices were prohibited by the Supreme Court as a violation of the doctrine of the separation of church and state, many schools substituted a "moment of silence." Some but not all of the state laws authorizing such moments of silence have also been struck down by the Court on the same legal grounds. Additionally, during the 1980s the Court disallowed invocations and blessings delivered by a member of the clergy at high school graduations.

Few cases decided by the Supreme Court have ever aroused the passions of the citizenry as much as the original school prayer case. Millions of Americans signed petitions calling for the impeachment of the Court's chief justice. Thirty-five years later, many people still find the decision shocking and view the Supreme Court as terribly misguided and out-of-step with American values. Politicians such as former President Ronald Reagan were fond of vilifying the decision and calling for a return of God and traditional values to the classroom. Citizens who favor school prayer have continued to be disappointed as new "conservative" justices appointed by Presidents Nixon, Bush, and Reagan continued and even extended the ban on prayer into new areas.

Ever since the original 1962 decision, efforts to pass a constitutional amendment to allow school prayer have been underway. These efforts have picked up momentum in recent years with the Republican party's "Contract with America," and they have the potential to move the issue of school prayer back to center stage in future elections.

Before the Supreme Court decisions, it was common for public schools to display Christmas and Easter decorations and to present Christmas and Easter pageants and music festivals. It was also somewhat common in parts of the country for schoolteachers to display a copy of the Ten Commandments in the classroom. The courts have also banned the display of religious symbols and activities in the public schools. This includes banning the singing of traditional Christmas carols in music classes. Although both Christmas and Easter have been commercialized by retailers, they are at root religious holidays, and the courts have held that celebration of such events using public tax dollars is a violation of the doctrine of the separation of church and state. Many Americans also disagree with this approach and see nothing wrong with such displays and activities.

Release Time Programs

Many public schools allow students to leave school early to attend religious instruction off school grounds. Although such programs are justified as an accommodation to religious students, others criticize them because they discriminate against nonreligious students and students of minority faiths who must remain at school with little to do while the released students are off taking religious instruction.

Access to Schools for Religious Groups

Although public schools are used primarily for the instruction of children, many districts allow other groups to rent or have free use of rooms after school hours for meetings. Separation of church and state issues arise when the public schools allow church-sponsored groups to use public school rooms. The issue is also raised when public school students wish to form Bible-reading groups or other religious-inspired clubs.

Flag Salutes and Compulsory Attendance

Members of certain religions object to reciting the pledge of allegiance. A number of court cases have considered the rights of these students when school authorities insist that all students recite the pledge. Similarly, the courts have had to resolve the issue of whether students can be required to attend school even when their religion forbids it.

Religion and Public School Curriculums

In 1925 the "Scopes Monkey Trial" received international attention, pitting those who supported the teaching of evolution against those who favored the biblical account of creation. John Scopes, a high school biology teacher, had defied the Tennessee law banning the teaching of evolution in public schools and universities. Although Scopes lost that trial, the issue was ultimately resolved in favor of the teaching of evolution in the public schools. In 1968 the Supreme Court ruled that the teaching of the biblical account of creation is the teaching of religious doctrine and inappropriate in the public schools. Although some readers might assume that this issue has been resolved, nothing is further from the truth.

The issue of teaching creationism along with teaching evolution is still a contemporary issue with vocal supporters on both sides. Despite the Supreme Court's ban on the teaching of creationism, many school districts require that "equal time" be given to evolution and "creation science." In fact, many biology teachers refrain from teaching evolution because it creates such a controversy with families who find it contrary to their religious beliefs. The controversy over the teaching of evolution is still simmering nationwide.

Another aspect of religion in the schools concerns the censorship of public school textbooks. Students receive much of their information from textbooks and these books play a significant role in students' developing views of the world. Some citizens are concerned not only about what is included and excluded but about how particular subjects are treated. The treatment of the theory of evolution and Darwin's *Origin of Species* is of course a controversial subject for textbooks. To avoid offending decisionmakers, some publishers minimize coverage in this area.

Textbooks are typically selected by school boards on the recommendation of teachers, although in some states, such as Texas, a state board makes the purchasing decisions and selects one approved text for each subject. Because few people get involved in trying to influence textbook adoption decisions, a small minority who exert pressure on the decisionmakers can have a disproportionate influence. Critics of textbooks normally point to the lack of emphasis on "family values" in these books. The teaching of evolution is not the only concern in the censorship area; critics also object to information on other subjects such as sex education, homosexuality, and AIDS. They object to books and readings that present ambiguous ethical situations in which right and wrong answers are not obvious. They argue that students are being taught "relative" values rather than the "firm" moral values laid out in scripture. They argue that the school systems are trying to replace Christianity with "secular humanism," which the critics see as the root of many of America's problems.

The controversy over the content of books also extends to library books. There are literally hundreds of challenges to school and public library books each year. In fact, school library books probably generate more controversy than school textbooks because textbook publishers tend to edit textbooks to minimize controversy and maximize adoptions and sales. Novels and nonfiction books have proven more controversial. Individuals and groups frequently object to the inclusion of books that don't "promote family values." Although sexual content is probably the most frequent complaint, library books are also attacked because they contain "objectionable language" or relativistic values.

Support for Church-affiliated Schools

The last major issue covered in this book involves public support for church-supported schools. The Supreme Court has ruled that students have a right to attend church-supported schools, and students have an option to attend parochial schools or to be schooled at home. Of course this option relieves the taxpayers of the cost of educating the students and subsidizes a basic government service. Governments have attempted to subsidize parochial and other church-supported schools not just for the purpose of assisting the students, but because the parochial schools help relieve the financial burden on the public schools. The courts have been asked to decide cases where the government has attempted to provide aid to church-supported schools on the theory that the aid is going to the children, not to the schools.

Governments have provided various types of aid. Over the years governments have attempted to pay teachers in parochial schools to teach basic academic subjects. More recently they have paid teachers to provide federally mandated special education services. Governments have also tried providing free textbooks to parochial school students, reasoning that the books go to the children, not the parochial schools. The provision of free bus transportation to parochial school children has also been challenged in the court cases.

The latest development in the area of aid to church-supported schools involves the use of "vouchers." Vouchers are issued by local governments to allow students to attend private schools including church-related schools. In effect, vouchers would allow tax dollars to be used to pay tuition at a secular private school or a church-supported private school. Vouchers have been attacked as a violation of the doctrine of the separation of church and state, but the issue has yet to be resolved and promises to be one of the more controversial aspects of religion in the schools.

I would like to thank my editors at ABC-CLIO for their help and encouragement in the development of this book. The views expressed in this book are my own and are not necessarily those of my university. Any errors are the sole responsibility of the author.

Introduction 1

Families of very different backgrounds come together in American public schools, often bringing very different values and religious beliefs. But schools also play a large role in shaping children's social values and worldview, and parents and others are rightfully concerned about the messages that children receive in the classroom. Although some parents object to any religious observance in the classroom, others feel that excluding religious activities and observances creates a "godless" atmosphere that has contributed to the moral decline of the citizenry.

Religion in the schools has also become an important national political issue. National legislators and presidential candidates have taken an interest in the topic, at least in part because it is an issue of prime interest to voters. Evidence suggests that Americans are in general apathetic about political issues—fewer than half of all eligible voters vote in most elections. Many Americans perceive that they have little control over decisions made in Washington, D.C. However, Americans do get more concerned over local issues that directly affect themselves and their families. No issue hits closer to home than that of religion in the schools.

1

This issue has a strong polarizing effect on society. Those who believe that religion has no place in public schools want to maintain the "wall of separation" erected by the courts that has banned school prayer, Christian observances, and the teaching of "creation science" in the schools. Those who believe that its exclusion ignores the reality that Americans are a religious people want to reinstate school prayer and Christmas festivals, and many also want the teaching of the biblical account of creation to be given equal treatment when teachers discuss the theory of evolution. Many Americans favor a constitutional amendment allowing prayer in public schools.

Diversity of Religion in America

The United States is notable for its religious pluralism. Although a majority of Americans describe themselves as Christians, there are a remarkable number of individual Christian churches with varying beliefs and doctrines. And, of course, there are millions of religious Americans who are not Christians—and millions more who profess no religious beliefs. Although the United States has always had a diverse population, the trend has accelerated. The insularity of small towns is eroding and migration and immigration have created a more heterogeneous mix of schoolchildren in many areas of the country. An increasing number of schoolchildren are non-Christian immigrants from Asian countries. These students' families not only speak diverse languages but are also members of diverse religions. Our governmental system is designed to protect the interests of these minorities as well as the interests of the majority.

Some Americans feel that efforts to accommodate religious minorities have gone too far and that these efforts have resulted in discrimination against the Christian majority. Specifically, they argue that the courts' approach of banning prayer and other religious activities in the schools is flawed, that this enforced "secularization" of the public schools in the interest of protecting the minority of believers and nonbelievers has impinged on the majority's right to religious expression. In their view, the schools need not be "godless," secular institutions, but public places where religious expression is tolerated and not suppressed. Their opponents argue that allowing organized prayer and other religious activity in the schools will be an unconstitutional promotion of the majority's religion at the expense of minority believers.

Historical Background

Diversity of religion has been a feature of American society since the colonial period. Indeed, many of the original thirteen colonies were populated by immigrants who were members of minority religious sects and fled England and other European nations to gain religious freedom. The original pattern of settlement segregated Puritans in the Massachusetts Bay Colony, Quakers in Pennsylvania, and Catholics in Maryland. Although these groups left their countries of origin because they were not allowed to freely practice their faith, they generally felt no obligation to afford religious tolerance to others. When these diverse groups found themselves bound together in the new nation called the United States, they had to devise ways to live together.

In the 1700s most European countries had an "established" church with close ties to the government. In all nations the established church received financial support from the government, and in many countries religious diversity was not tolerated. For example, the king of France expelled the Protestant Huguenots, who eventually made their way to Nova Scotia and then on to Louisiana. (Their travails were the subject of the dramatic poem "Evangeline" by Henry Wadsworth Longfellow.) The new American republic, made up of groups of diverse religions, rejected the concept of an established church. Because of the colonists' religious diversity it is unlikely that they could have achieved any consensus. Instead, the Americans created a governmental system that would protect and promote the original religious diversity of the country. Today, Americans enjoy almost unrestrained opportunity to freely practice the religion of their choice.

Freedom of Religion

Religious freedom has always been recognized as an important individual right in America, and that right is enshrined in the First Amendment of the U.S. Constitution: "Congress shall make no law respecting an establishment of religion, or prohibiting the free exercise thereof."

The first half of this First Amendment guarantee of freedom of religion is called the "establishment clause" and guarantees that the government will not create an established church. The second half, called the "free exercise clause," prohibits the government from enacting laws that impinge on any individual's practice of religion. The U.S. Supreme Court has firmly established that the

First Amendment protections also apply to limit the actions of state and local governments, including public schools.

Although the language of the First Amendment's freedom of religion guarantee is succinct and precise, it has engendered endless disputes and hundreds of court cases over the years. On a literal level, the First Amendment may appear only to limit the establishment of an "official" church. However, the courts have held that any favoritism on the part of the schools can be a violation of the establishment clause. Posting of the Ten Commandments has been held to be contrary to the establishment clause because it favors Christianity and Judaism over other religions. Daily in-class recitation of the Lord's Prayer favors Christianity. The courts have held that even permitting a moment of silence in the classroom to encourage individual prayer can be unconstitutional. On the other hand, the Supreme Court has also recognized that religious students do have a constitutional right to religious expression that does not end at the schoolhouse door. Students may use school facilities for religiously oriented clubs. They may also engage in silent prayer and student-inspired vocal prayer.

Most agree with the concept of religious freedom, but the actual application of that guarantee has generated a lot of controversy. The First Amendment itself creates an inherent difficulty. Although the establishment clause requires that government cannot endorse a specific religion or the practice of a specific religion, the free exercise clause also requires that the government do nothing to discourage individual religious practice and expression.

When the government bans religious activity, such as Bible reading, from the schools in an effort to comply with the establishment clause, it certainly limits the rights of the individuals who wish to read the Bible in school. On the other hand, if the courts permit the Bible reading to promote the free exercise of religion, they are implicitly endorsing the practice of a particular religion in violation of the establishment clause. The First Amendment creates two freedom of religion goals that are sometimes impossible to reconcile.

Separation of Church and State

Religion in the schools has to be viewed in the larger context of the separation of church and state. The founding fathers envisioned a secular government. Religion and politics were to be separate spheres. The founders clearly recognized that freedom of religion required that government not be involved in the promotion or protection of particular faiths or the discouraging of citizens from practicing particular faiths.

To be sure, the separation of church and state in America has never been complete. From the earliest days of the republic, the president has taken the oath of office by swearing on the Bible, and it is the custom in many courts for witnesses to do the same. Our currency bears the motto "In God We Trust," although interestingly this custom only started during the twentieth century. The pledge of allegiance includes the words "One nation under God," although the words "under God" were added during the 1950s in the Cold War period. Churches pay no local property taxes. Despite these entanglements, it is clear that the founding fathers recognized that to preserve freedom of religion, religion and politics had to be separated.

Despite this strict separation of church and state, many important political decisions have ethical and religious implications, some obvious, some more subtle. For example, whether a city can erect a cross on city property obviously raises the question of the city promoting or endorsing Christianity. Although the majority of the citizens may view the activity as a praiseworthy use of tax money, it may offend those of other faiths or those of no faith. This issue is at once both a political and a religious issue. The legality of abortion is another issue that has obvious religious implications.

The religious aspects of an issue may sometimes be less obvious. For example, gays in the military may appear to be a political or social issue, but it also can be viewed as a religious one. Hostility toward the gay lifestyle may be rooted in individual religious belief. Some persons may believe that the Bible condemns homosexuality and that it should not be tolerated or encouraged in any way. Although our political system is based on the separation of church and state, issues are not always clearly secular or religious. Because of this overlap it may be difficult to separate religion and politics. Not surprisingly, these issues that have both political and religious implications are the very issues that evoke the greatest passion.

Key Conflict Areas

There are six major conflict areas involving religion and the schools: (1) school prayer and other in-school religious activities; (2) release time programs; (3) access to schools for religious groups; (4) flag salutes and compulsory attendance; (5) religion and public school curriculums; and (6) support for church-affiliated schools.

School Prayer and Other Religious Activities

Prayer and other in-school religious activities has been the most divisive aspect of religion in the schools. In colonial times the schools were largely operated by the churches and prayer and religion were daily features of the school day. In later times when the schools were operated by local school boards and supported by local taxes, religious activities continued. Daily prayer and Bible recitation were universal. As nineteenth-century immigration made the U.S. population more diverse, friction arose over the recitation of Protestant prayers and readings from the King James Bible in the public schools. In 1910, the Illinois Supreme Court banned in-class reading of the King James Bible in the Chicago public schools. However, in most parts of the country, prayer and Bible reading in the schools continued despite occasional complaints.

In 1962 and 1963 the U.S. Supreme Court heard two cases in which parents claimed that organized school prayer violated the First Amendment's protection against the establishment of religion. The Supreme Court agreed with the parents and banned organized prayer from the public schools nationwide in one of the most important and far-reaching cases ever heard by the Supreme Court. *Engel v. Vitale* (1962), decided by a 6-to-3 vote, declared unconstitutional a short, innocuous-sounding, nondenominational school prayer written by the New York State Board of Regents (an administrative body overseeing quality in the New York state public schools). The prayer was intended to be inoffensive to those who were compelled to recite it: "Almighty God, we acknowledge our dependence upon Thee, and we beg Thy blessings upon us, our parents, our teachers and our Country." But the Supreme Court found the government-written prayer impermissible under the Constitution. Justice Hugo Black wrote for the Court that it is "no part of the business of government to compose official prayers."

Engel v. Vitale is an interesting decision for a number of reasons. Although six judges concurred, there was one dissent and two justices did not participate. Generally, decisions with less than the full Court participating create a less powerful precedent. This case proved the exception to the rule: It created a powerful precedent for the Supreme Court and lower federal and state courts as well. The case was a virtual bombshell, triggering banner headlines worldwide. The political firestorm should not have been unexpected. Prayer and Bible reading was an established routine in many if not most schools, and many people couldn't comprehend why the Court would ban the practice if a majority of the community wanted it. Although a majority of Americans might have wanted prayer in the public schools, constitutional protections are not only for the majority—they exist to protect minority interests.

Generations of Americans had grown up with school prayer. Religious Americans took the decision as a personal rebuke. The decision also had a tremendous polarizing political effect. Those who supported the rights of minorities—especially non-Christians—hailed the decision as progressive. They pointed out that the decision did not eliminate any student's right to pray silently or aloud in school. It merely banned public schools from composing and compelling the recitation of prayers. Critics of the decision labeled the court and justices as godless or communists.

A year later the Supreme Court heard another major school prayer case, *Abington School District v. Schempp* (1963) and again declared that organized prayer had no place in the public schools. The case went even further than *Engel v. Vitale*. The 1963 school prayer case banned both the recitation of the Lord's Prayer and Bible reading in public schools.

As in the prior year, the decision caused a furor. This was fueled in part because one of the companion cases before the high court—*Murray v. Curlett*—was brought by Madalyn Murray, an avowed atheist and communist and pro-Castro supporter. The timing could not have been worse. The United States had just emerged from the Cuban missile crisis—a showdown between President Kennedy and Nikita Krushchev of the Soviet Union over the placement of hostile missiles in Cuba—just ninety miles from Florida. President Kennedy had just committed troops to South Vietnam to combat communist incursions. Many Americans were thus ready to believe that the school prayer case was more evidence of godless, communist influences within the United States.

Opposition to the banning of school prayer was swift. Criticism was leveled at the Supreme Court's opinion from politicians and also from the pulpit. Groups such as the right-wing John Birch Society organized a campaign to impeach Chief Justice Earl Warren who wrote the majority opinion. An amendment to allow school prayer was placed before Congress. In fact amendments to allow school prayer have been introduced in almost every Congress for 25 years but have never come close to being enacted. Despite the ruling, many public schools—especially in the South—continue today to have either Bible reading or a school prayer at the start of the day in defiance of the Court's ban.

The ban on school prayer also included a ban on prayers said at graduations and sports events. A divided Supreme Court, in *Lee v. Weisman* 505 U.S. 577 (1992), ruled that an invocation at a public school graduation ceremony in Providence, Rhode Island, violated the establishment clause. Justice Anthony Kennedy, writing for the majority, argued that the public atmosphere created an improper coercion on students, which amounted to proselytizing. The majority opinion held that since the graduation ceremony was a required event, a prayer at the graduation was no more acceptable than a prayer in the classroom at the start of the school day. Justice Antonin Scalia wrote a bitter dissent accusing the majority of "laying waste" to traditional nonsectarian prayers at public events and accused the majority's use of "coercion" to be a "bulldozer of its social engineering."

Despite the ban on school prayer, states have sometimes tried to reintroduce prayer through legislation. For example, Mississippi enacted a law allowing student-initiated voluntary prayer at all assemblies, sporting events, commencement exercises, and other school-related events. The law was passed after an incident at a Mississippi high school. A high school principal had allowed a student to recite a daily prayer over the school public address system. When some parents complained, the board of education threatened to fire the principal. Many Mississippians are strongly religious and favor school prayer, and the entire episode caused a local furor. This prompted the legislature to pass the law. The law was immediately challenged by the ACLU, and a Mississippi federal district judge upheld the section of the law allowing prayers at commencement exercises but struck down the parts of the act allowing prayer at assemblies and other school-related events (*Ingebretsem v. Jackson Public School District*). A few states still have laws in effect that allow school prayer. These laws might be challenged in court. For an overview of specific state laws concerning prayer in the schools, see Table 1.1.

Prayer in the public schools continues to be a contentious issue. Both federal and state courts have almost always struck down compulsory and voluntary group prayers in public schools

TABLE 1.1
Prayer in Public Schools

State	Code Section	Provisions
Alabama	16-1-20.1, *et seq.*	Period of silence not to exceed one minute in duration, shall be observed for meditation or voluntary prayer, and during any such period no other activities shall be engaged in
Alaska	No statutory provisions	
Arizona	15-522	One minute period of silence for meditation
Arkansas	6-16-119	Brief period of silent meditation and reflection
California	No statutory provisions	
Colorado	No statutory provisions	
Connecticut	10-16a	Silent meditation
Delaware	Tit. 14 §4101	Two to three minutes to voluntarily participate in moral, philosophical, patriotic, or religious activity
District of Columbia	No statutory provisions	
Florida	233.062	Brief period not to exceed two minutes, for the purpose of silent prayer or meditation
Georgia	20-2-1050	Brief period of silent prayer or meditation
Hawaii	No statutory provisions	
Idaho	No statutory provisions	
Illinois	105 ILCS 20/1	Brief period of silence which shall not be conducted as a religious exercise but shall be an opportunity for silent prayer or for silent reflection
Indiana	20-10.1-7-11	Brief period of silent prayer or meditation
Iowa	No statutory provisions	
Kansas	72-5308a	Brief period of silence to be used as opportunity for silent prayer or for silent reflection
Kentucky	158.175	Recitation of Lord's prayer to teach our country's history and as an affirmation of the freedom of religion in this country
Louisiana	17:2115(A)	Brief time of silent meditation
Maine	Tit. 20-A, §4805	Period of silence shall be observed for reflection or meditation
Maryland	Educ. §7-104	Meditate silently for approximately one minute; student or teacher may read the holy scriptures or pray
Massachusetts	Ch. 71 §1A	Period of silence not to exceed one minute in duration shall be observed for personal thoughts

(continues)

TABLE 1.1 (continued)

State	Code Section	Provisions
Michigan	§380.1565	Opportunity to observe time in silent meditation
Minnesota	No statutory provisions	
Mississippi	37-13-4	Teacher may permit the voluntary participation by students or others in prayer
Missouri	No statutory provisions	
Montana	20-7-112	Any teacher, principal, or superintendent may open the school day with a prayer
Nebraska	No statutory provisions	
Nevada	No statutory provisions	
New Hampshire	189:1-b	Period of not more than five minutes shall be available to those who wish to exercise their right to freedom of assembly and participate voluntarily in the free exercise of religion
New Jersey	18A:36-4	Observe a one-minute period of silence to be used solely at the discretion of the individual student for quiet and private contemplation or introspection
New Mexico	22-5-4.1	Period of silence not to exceed one minute to be used for contemplation, meditation, or prayer; held to be unconstitutional: *Duffy v. Las Cruces Public Schools*, 557 F. Supp 1013
New York	Educ. §3029-a	Brief period of silent meditation which may be opportunity for silent meditation on a religious theme or silent reflection
North Carolina	No statutory provisions	
North Dakota	15-47-30.1	Period of silence not to exceed one minute for meditation or prayer
Ohio	3313.601	Reasonable periods of time for programs or meditation upon a moral, philosophical, or patriotic theme
Oklahoma	11-101.1	Shall permit those students and teachers who wish to do so to participate in voluntary prayer
Oregon	No statutory provisions	
Pennsylvania	Tit. 24§15-1516.1	Brief period of silent prayer or meditation which is not a religious exercise but an opportunity for prayer or reflection as child is disposed
Rhode Island	16-12-3.1	Period of silence not to exceed one minute in duration shall be observed for meditation

TABLE 1.1 (continued)

State	Code Section	Provisions
South Carolina	No statutory provisions	
South Dakota	No statutory provisions	
Tennessee	49-6-1004(a)	Mandatory period of silence of approximately one minute
Texas	No statutory provisions	
Utah	No statutory provisions	
Vermont	No statutory provisions	
Virginia	22.1-203	School may establish the daily observance of one minute of silence
Washington	No statutory provisions	
West Virginia	Const. Art. III, §15A	Designated brief time for students to exercise their right to personal and private contemplation, meditation, etc.
Wisconsin	No statutory provisions	
Wyoming	No statutory provisions	

Source: *National Survey of State Laws,* pp. 160–161. Edited by Richard A. Leiter. Copyright © 1993 Gale Research. All rights reserved. Reproduced by permission.

as contrary to the U.S. Constitution's establishment clause, which bars the government from favoring one religion over another. Many have argued that the courts have gone too far by banning school prayer. They argue that the establishment clause only requires that the government be neutral toward religion by not favoring one church or religion over another, and that by enacting an outright ban on school prayer the government is being hostile rather than neutral toward religious practice. These proponents also argue that by banning school prayer, the government has also limited the right of students and teachers to practice their religion. Those who support this view argue that the courts need to make a reasonable accommodation to those who want to express their religious practices during the day.

On the other hand, there are many who feel that allowing any kind of prayer in the schools—even a supposedly nondenominational prayer—constitutes overt support of religion in violation of the establishment clause's wall of separation between church and state. These proponents would argue that students have the constitutional right to be free from a particular religion or free from all religion. By requiring a mandatory school prayer, students and teachers who do not wish to practice religion have their rights violated.

Individual school districts and state legislators have seized upon the idea of allowing a moment of silence before the start of the school day as a substitute for a group prayer. At the high school level this moment is typically observed in the homeroom before classes begin. The goal is to allow students and teachers to pray silently or to meditate. The legality of such moments of silence depends on their intent: If they are really moments for prayer then they are illegal.

For example, the Supreme Court, in *Wallace v. Jaffree* (1985), invalidated an Alabama law allowing a one-minute period of silence at the start of each school day "for meditation or voluntary prayer." A divided court (6 to 3) concluded that this mandated moment of silence amounted to "the State's endorsement of prayer activity" that transgressed the proper wall of separation between church and state. Merely allowing students to be excused was held insufficient to save the law. The Court did say, however, that it was possible for a moment of silence to pass muster if it was not solely for sectarian purposes. The problem with the Alabama law was that it was avowedly for prayer. Presumably a statute that required a moment of silence for no reason would have avoided the constitutional problems. Of course, the Supreme Court has never prohibited prayer in the public schools. Students are free to pray silently or out loud. However, the school cannot conduct religious ceremonies, including the recitation of prayers in the classroom.

Although teacher-organized prayer in the schools is illegal, a student can silently pray at any time. Accordingly, a properly devised moment of silence will withstand a legal challenge. The key is for the law to avoid outright religious intent. For example, Georgia enacted a "moment of quiet reflection" that allows public school teachers to begin the school day. Although the practice was immediately attacked as a "silent prayer," the Georgia silent moment law was upheld by a federal court because the law establishing the moment specifically disclaimed any religious purpose. Accordingly, the federal district court held that the law did not violate the Constitution *(Bown v. Gwinnett School District)*.

Today about half the states have a law specifically authorizing a moment of silence at the start of the school day. Some of these are probably legal while others may be found illegal if challenged. Those in favor of the moment of silence argue that it is a reasonable accommodation of those students and teachers who wish to practice their religion by praying in school without offending or inconveniencing those who do not wish to participate. Those who are opposed argue that the school districts are sneaking prayer into the schools through the back door. Those who oppose the moment of silence also argue that students and teachers are free to pray silently to themselves at any time during the school day.

The U.S. Supreme Court's position on the moment of silence has been neutral, but its decisions have led to confusion in this area. The Supreme Court's position is that the constitutionality of a moment of silence depends on the wording and the intent of the state statute. If the intent of the statute is to encourage and promote prayer, then the moment of silence is unconstitutional. However, if the intent is not to actively promote prayer then the moment of silence would pass constitutional muster. In the 1985 case, *Wallace v. Jaffree*, described above, which involved Alabama's moment of silence statute, the Court struck down the Alabama law because the state legislature's intent was to promote and encourage prayer in the public schools.

Other states and individual school districts have also adopted moments of silence. Because school prayer is such a contentious issue the subject has also become a political issue. Some elected officials oppose the moment of silence; even more seem to favor it. A number of U.S. presidents—including President Bill Clinton—have endorsed the moment of silence concept as a reasonable accommodation of religious practice. They argue, possibly for reasons of voter popularity, that banning the moment of silence shows not neutrality but an active hostility to any religious practice in the schools.

Other religious activities in the schools, such as the posting of the Lord's Prayer or Ten Commandments or the singing of hymns, are normally impermissible using the same logic applied in the school prayer cases, that allowing such religious activities in state-supported schools is an unconstitutional endorsement of a particular religion. Christmas pageants and decorations are also viewed with suspicion, although a few courts have ruled that both Thanksgiving and Christmas have become secular and commercialized holidays and are no longer purely religious. For example, singing the song "Rudolph the Red-nosed Reindeer" has no religious significance. But some might argue that any reference to Christmas is an endorsement of religion.

Release Time

Release time has been one of the most litigated areas of religion in the schools. Release time (also called dismissed time) is a program in which a public school dismisses students early to attend religion classes away from the public school grounds. Originally the schools allowed the classes to be taught in regular public school classrooms. Today, classes typically are offered at individual churches and children attend the classes at the church at which they regularly worship. Parents may give permission to the public school for their children to be released early for such classes. If parental permission is not given the children are required to stay at the public school.

Release time programs were upheld by the U.S. Supreme Court in *Zorach v. Clauson* (1952). Earlier release time programs, in which religion classes were taught in public school classrooms during the release time period, were struck down by the Supreme Court as a violation of the establishment clause in *Illinois ex. rel McCollum v. Board of Education* (1948). In the *McCollum* case, although the religion teachers were not paid or selected by the public, school administrators could veto the selection of teachers, and the Supreme Court felt that the "use of the state's compulsory school machinery" to disseminate religious doctrines violated the separation of church and state.

Vashti McCollum gained the national spotlight when she filed a lawsuit objecting to the religion classes being given in her son's school. A local group, the Council on Religious Education, was formed to provide religious instruction in the Champaign, Illinois, school system. The students were released early from class and children with parental permission attended religion classes in their own schools. Nearly all the children participated and instruction was available for Jews, Catholics, and Protestants. Although McCollum had given her son Terry permission to attend the classes when he was in fourth grade, she grew uncomfortable with the instruction and did not give permission the next year. Although her son was not compelled to attend, he was required to sit alone in a small anteroom outside the teacher's restroom or to sit alone in the hall. He was the subject of teasing from his fellow students and disapproval from his teachers. When the school district failed to improve the situation, McCollum sued.

The U.S. Supreme Court agreed with McCollum, holding that the teaching of religion on the school grounds violated the First Amendment's establishment clause. Following on the footsteps of *Everson v. Board of Education* (1947) from the previous year, which held that state and local governments, including the public schools, were subject to the establishment clause, the Court used its power of judicial review to invalidate the state law that established the release time program. No federal or state law can be contrary to a constitutional provision. Although declaring laws contrary to the Constitution is a judicial power, judicial review also gives the Supreme Court a vast power to control how the law is applied in a particular area. The effect of *McCollum* was not only to outlaw the Illinois program but any existing or potential programs that suffered from the same defects. The *McCollum* case really set the stage for all of the later cases that banned religious expression in the public schools. McCollum later wrote that she paid a personal price for her beliefs—that she and her family were harassed during the legal proceedings.

In 1952 the Court considered another release time case, *Zorach v. Clauson* 343 U.S. 306. This time the Supreme Court upheld the release time program, which was taking place outside public school grounds. The release time program was structured to allow public school students to be dismissed early to attend religion classes away from the public school grounds. Parents could give permission to the public school for their children to be released early for such classes. If permission was not granted the children were required to stay at the public school. The Court clearly felt more comfortable with the classes being held off the school premises, although the school system assisted the programs by helping with registration and permitting the students to leave school. Justice William O. Douglas's opinion noted that, although it was clear that the First Amendment required a separation of church and state, it was equally clear that the establishment clause did not require "a philosophy of hostility to religion" but "respects the religious nature of our people and accommodates the public service to their spiritual needs." Three justices wrote dissenting opinions noting that there was not much to distinguish this case from the 1948 *McCollum* case that had disapproved of release time programs and that the fact that in this case the children attended the classes at church rather than in the school itself seemed trivial to the dissenters.

Today release time programs remain a feature of American education. Proponents of release time programs argue that they are a reasonable accommodation of religion that fall just short of endorsement. Opponents argue that release time programs discriminate against both nonreligious students and students whose religions cannot provide them with a program during the release time. Those students must usually sit in study halls during the release time period. Opponents argue that they are merely being warehoused so that the majority of students can go to religious instruction during the school day. These opponents argue that if students and their parents want religious instruction it should be done after school or on weekends, not during the normal school day.

Access for Religious Groups

After the school prayer case, *Engel v. Vitale* (1962), which declared the New York Regents' nondenominational school prayer unconstitutional, many schools reacted by banning all religious activities in the schools. In addition to terminating in-school release time programs, school boards also banned student religious clubs and after-school Bible study groups. Parents complained that this amounted to discrimination against religious students who had a constitutional right to express their religious beliefs and to associate with one another.

In response, Congress passed the federal Equal Access Act, which prohibits discrimination against student groups on the basis of religious, political, or philosophical views. If a public school allows other "non-curriculum related groups" (other clubs) to use its facilities, then the school must give equal access to those facilities to religious groups. The act was controversial from the start—some asserted that allowing religious clubs in the schools would violate the establishment clause by favoring one particular religion.

The legality of the Equal Access Act was tested in *Board of Education of the Westside Community Schools v. Mergens* (1980), and the Court upheld the constitutionality of the federal Equal Access Act. Relying on the *Lemon* test, a three-step test from *Lemon v. Kurtzman* (1971) used to judge the validity of state aid to religion, the Supreme Court held that a public school district must allow students access to school facilities for a religious club. Under the Equal Access Act, public schools that receive federal aid and provide a "limited open forum" cannot deny equal access to students who wish to meet together in a religious club. The Court held that although there was some involvement of school officials in the appealed cases, this did not amount to prohibited "entanglement" with religion nor an endorsement of any particular religion. Clearly, changes of personnel on the Court over the years had made a difference; if this case had been brought two decades earlier, the Court would have found the entire act unconstitutional.

The Court has also ruled that nonstudent religious groups can use the public schools. In *Lamb's Chapel v. Center Moriches School District* (1993), the Supreme Court held that a school district cannot deny access to school facilities to a church group that wants to show a film on child rearing. This school district had rented space to other groups for secular activities but had denied access to the religious group out of concern over promoting religion at the school. Although the film was shown only to the church group and after school hours, the Court held that any benefit to the group was merely "incidental."

Proponents of equal access to public school facilities argue that religious clubs should be treated no differently than other school clubs. They argue that to do otherwise would amount to discrimination against religion and would also infringe on the First Amendment right to free speech and freedom of association. Opponents argue that the schools cannot be used for religious clubs because this amounts to an implicit endorsement of a particular religion by the school. They also argue that this will inevitably discriminate against students who are members of minority religions who will have no opportunity to participate in a club of their choice because there would be too few students.

Flag Salutes and Compulsory School Attendance

The pledge of allegiance has generated some of the most intense conflicts involving religion in the schools. Students at the start of each school day have traditionally recited the patriotic pledge of allegiance, although today its recitation is becoming less common in some parts of the country. Interestingly, the words "under God" were inserted in the pledge only in 1954 (and before World War II, students saluted the flag using what would become the familiar Nazi salute). The Jehovah's Witnesses prohibit their members from reciting the pledge because they believe it to be worship of a "graven image." Quakers also are uncomfortable with the word "pledge," and an early concession was made. The presidential oath of office allows the president the option to "affirm" or to "pledge" to uphold the duties of president.

During World War II the recitation of the pledge became mandatory at the start of every school day as the United States prepared to enter the war. Parents of Jehovah's Witness students sued to allow their children to avoid recitation of the pledge on religious grounds, but the U.S. Supreme Court held in *Minersville School District v. Gobitis* (1940) that Jehovah's Witnesses cannot be excused from reciting the pledge of allegiance in school. Justice Felix Frankfurter, writing for the Court, held that despite the fact that their religious precepts prohibited reciting the pledge, the government could force schoolchildren to recite the pledge of allegiance to create national unity. The date of the case is important. Frankfurter, a brilliant ex–law professor, had immigrated to the United States as a child with his Jewish parents. Frankfurter was fervently patriotic and undoubtedly believed that reciting the pledge was a small price to pay for the privilege of living in the United States, despite objections on religious grounds. The 8-to-1 Court decision caused many school boards to expel Jehovah's Witness children from school and even precipitated mob violence against Witness churches, some of which were burned. Some people viewed the Jehovah's Witnesses' refusals to recite the pledge as treason rather than as a sincere expression of religious beliefs.

The decision of the Court didn't stand for long. In *Virginia State Board of Education v. Barnette* 319 U.S. 624 (1943), the Supreme Court ruled unconstitutional a West Virginia law requiring mandatory recitals of the pledge of allegiance and flag salutes in public schoolrooms. Three new members had been added to the Court since *Gobitis,* and two justices had changed their minds about the issue.

In *Cantwell v. Connecticut* (1940), the Supreme Court accepted another case involving two Jehovah's Witnesses who sought to pass out religious literature in downtown New Haven, Connecticut. New Haven had passed a law requiring those who wished to pass out religious literature to get a license. The law's purpose was to discourage and regulate Jehovah's Witnesses and other groups. The Cantwells did not apply for a license because they presumed they would be turned down on the grounds that they were not members of an established religion. In dicta the Court noted that freedom of religion includes the freedom to believe and the freedom to act, and that the first is an absolute right while the second is not. The case is also notable because for the first time the Supreme Court ruled that the free exercise clause of the First Amendment not only applies to the federal government but also to the states, and, accordingly, to the actions of local school districts. The Cantwells carried a portable spring-loaded phonograph on which they played a record called "Enemies," which was a diatribe against other religions—especially the

Roman Catholic church. Catholic passersby were angered and threatened the Cantwells with physical violence if they didn't leave. Although they left without incident, the local police arrested them and charged them with inciting a breach of the peace and evangelizing without the required license.

The Supreme Court also found the license requirement a prohibited prior restraint. The local law put the local authorities in charge of determining what was a religion. Although New Haven could control street activity, allowing local authorities to decide what speakers and activities to permit was an impermissible burden on the free exercise of religion.

To avoid the secular nature of the public schools, many parents prefer to have their children educated in private religious schools or educated at home. The constitutional ban on school prayer and other religious activities only applies to government-supported public schools, not to private schools. The issue of compulsory education has caused a number of problems over the years. Parents did not always have the right to school their children outside of the public school system. During the 1920s, Oregon voters, alarmed at the growing number of Catholics and Catholic schools in their midst, passed a referendum that amended the state constitution to require all schoolchildren to attend only public schools. Private and parochial schools were to be outlawed. At the time, Ku Klux Klan activity was strong in Oregon, and the law was directly aimed at the Roman Catholic church school system. But the law also affected other private schools as well as parochial schools. The Catholic church and several private schools challenged the law and the case eventually made its way to the U.S. Supreme Court.

In 1925, in *Pierce v. Society of Sisters*, the Supreme Court struck down Oregon's compulsory education law that required all students to attend public school. The case held that parents have the right to send their children to a nonpublic school. This case still stands to support the view that church schools and home schooling can be an alternative to the public school system for those parents who want their children to be schooled in a religious atmosphere.

The issue of religious beliefs and compulsory school attendance reached the Supreme Court again fifty years later. In *Yoder v. Wisconsin* (1972), the Supreme Court held it unconstitutional to require compulsory education for Old Order Amish children whose parents object on religious grounds. In *Yoder*, an 8-to-1 decision, the Court upheld the right of Amish parents to withhold their children from public school despite the state of Wisconsin's compulsory schooling law. The Court ruled that, although the state has a strong interest in requiring children to attend school, this does not overbalance the restraint on religious freedom of compelling them to attend school. The *Yoder* decision is unusual because it granted the Amish the free exercise of their beliefs despite a clear state law compelling school attendance. It is also a curious decision because it favored only that particular religious group.

These issues are extremely important ones because a large number of Christian parents now desire to educate their children outside the public school system in a religious atmosphere at Christian schools or in home schooling. This movement has created a potential conflict between the parents and state school authorities who are empowered to enforce educational standards in the schools. State officials must balance the right of parents to educate their children outside the public school system with the state's legitimate interest in ensuring that all children get a proper education. The states can prescribe the content of the materials used in private schools and in home schooling. For example, a state might challenge a Christian school or parent who refused to teach the theory of evolution. Because of the rise of Christian schools and home schooling, this area promises to be a contentious one in the next decade.

Religion and Public School Curriculums

Although school prayer cases make headline news, curriculum issues have also created their share of controversy. For example, many Christians dispute the validity of Darwin's theory of evolution, believing in the literal truth of the biblical account of the creation and objecting to the teaching of evolution in the schools. On the other hand, many other parents object to the teaching of the biblical account as the inappropriate teaching of religious dogma in the public schools. This is one issue where there is little middle ground, and today the pendulum has clearly swung in favor of evolution. But individual school districts and state governments continue to try to devise ways to allow the teaching of creationism in the schools. The issue, familiar to many people through the 1950s movie *Inherit the Wind,* is based on the famous Scopes trial.

The world watched the Scopes trial as noted attorney Clarence Darrow represented high school biology teacher John Thomas Scopes, who was charged with violating a Tennessee law prohibiting the teaching of evolution in the public schools. William Jennings Bryan defended the law for the state. Although Scopes was convicted and fined $100, the fine was thrown out on appeal. Bryan, a prime backer of antievolution laws, died just days after the trial. However, the conflict of evolution versus creationism lived on. Various states allowed, or even required, the teaching of the biblical account of creation alongside evolution or in place of it.

A few states had even banned the teaching of evolution because it ran counter to the biblical account of creation. In *Epperson v. Arkansas* (1985), the Supreme Court, in a unanimous opinion, struck down an Arkansas state statute that prohibited the teaching of evolution. The Court ruled that the ban was enacted entirely to "aid, foster, or promote one religious theory" over another and that it thereby violated the establishment clause of the First Amendment and that Arkansas could not require that its school curriculum be shaped to conform to the beliefs of a religion. After the Supreme Court prohibited states from banning the teaching of evolution in *Epperson,* creationists started labeling their body of information supporting the biblical version of creation as "creation science."

The teaching of creation science in the public schools does persist. But, after *Epperson,* it was unclear whether a school district could teach evolution and creation science side by side. Seventy years ago, the Louisiana legislature passed the Balanced Treatment for Creation-Science and Evolution-Science in Public School Instruction Act (1928), which mandates that any school teaching evolution must also provide equal classroom time to the teaching of creation science. Although applauded by religious leaders, the law was immediately challenged. But in *Edwards v. Aguillard* (1986), the Supreme Court invalidated the Louisiana act, ruling that the primary purpose for the law was to promote the teachings of Christianity and that this favoritism violated the establishment clause.

Although the courts have consistently struck down the teaching of creationism as contrary to the Constitution, proponents continue to actively lobby for its inclusion in curriculums. Conservative Christians have been successful in lobbying both publishers and school boards on textbook content. Because textbooks are sold nationally, publishers are reluctant to offend a significant number of parents. Accordingly, biology textbooks contain only a limited discussion of evolution and many also contain a reference to the biblical account of creation. Conservative Christians also lobby school boards to adopt textbooks and readers that promote so-called traditional family values. They strongly object to readings that adopt a "relativistic" approach to problems and lobby for materials that illustrate moral values and situations that have clear right and wrong answers. For an overview of the number and types of challenges to textbooks and library books, see Tables 1.2a, b, and c.

Public Support for Church-Affiliated Schools

Although the doctrine of the separation of church and state would seem to bar the provision of government aid for private church-affiliated schools, the legislatures and courts have recognized a number of exceptions for very practical reasons. The

TABLE 1.2a

Challenges to School Curriculum or School Library Texts, 1994–1995

State	Number of Challenges	State	Number of Challenges
California	44	Nevada	5
Texas	28	Oklahoma	5
Pennsylvania	27	Arkansas	4
Oregon	23	Connecticut	4
Georgia	20	Kentucky	4
Ohio	20	Maine	4
Washington	20	North Carolina	4
Michigan	19	Rhode Island	4
Minnesota	18	Tennessee	4
Florida	16	Idaho	3
New Hampshire	15	Louisiana	3
Iowa	13	Mississippi	3
Kansas	12	New Jersey	3
South Carolina	12	Utah	3
Wisconsin	12	Wyoming	3
Virginia	11	Delaware	2
Arizona	10	Montana	2
Indiana	10	North Dakota	2
Missouri	10	Vermont	2
New York	10	West Virginia	2
Massachusetts	9	Nebraska	1
Maryland	9	New Mexico	1
Colorado	6	South Dakota	1
Alabama	5	Hawaii	0
Alaska	5	District of Columbia	0
Illinois	5		

Source: People for the American Way, *Attacks on the Freedom to Learn* (1996). Reprinted by permission.

TABLE 1.2b
Most Frequently Challenged Books and Materials, 1994–1995

More Scary Stories to Tell in the Dark, Alvin Schwartz
Scary Stories to Tell in the Dark, Alvin Schwartz
I Know Why the Caged Bird Sings, Maya Angelou
Schindler's List, Steven Spielberg
The Giver, Lois Lowery
Scary Stories 3: More Tales to Chill Your Bones, Alvin Schwartz
Halloween ABC, Eve Meriam
Values and Choices [sex education materials]
Seventeen magazine
Bridge to Terabithia, Katherine Paterson
The Chocolate War, Robert Cormier
Of Mice and Men, John Steinbeck
My Brother Sam Is Dead, Christopher and James Lincoln Collier

Source: People for the American Way, *Attacks on the Freedom to Learn* (1996). Reprinted by permission.

TABLE 1.2c
Most Frequently Challenged Authors, 1982–1995

Judy Blume	Robert Cormier	Mark Twain
Alvin Schwartz	J. D. Salinger	Katherine Paterson
Stephen King	Roald Dahl	Maya Angelou
John Steinbeck		

Most Frequently Challenged Books, 1982–1995

Of Mice and Men, John Steinbeck
The Catcher in the Rye, J. D. Salinger
Scary Stories to Tell in the Dark, Alvin Schwartz
The Chocolate War, Robert Cormier
More Scary Stories to Tell in the Dark, Alvin Schwartz
The Adventures of Huckleberry Finn, Mark Twain
I Know Why the Caged Bird Sings, Maya Angelou
Go Ask Alice, anonymous
Bridge to Terabithia, Katherine Paterson
The Witches, Roald Dahl

Most Frequently Challenged Films, 1982–1995

Romeo and Juliet
Schindler's List

Source: People for the American Way, *Attacks on the Freedom to Learn* (1996). Reprinted by permission.

courts justify these exceptions by holding that the aid goes to the schoolchildren and not to the private schools.

As mentioned above, the U.S. Supreme Court held in *Pierce v. Society of Sisters* (1925) that the Fourteenth Amendment protected students' rights to attend private schools. However, the high court has never held that government tax dollars could contribute to their support. In other countries—including Canada—government tax dollars are used to support parochial schools. In the United States, such support is avoided because of our doctrine of the separation of church and state, mandated not only by long tradition but also by the U.S. Constitution.

Many parents prefer to send their children to church-affiliated schools, and many of these parents feel that their tax dollars should be used to help support those schools. Local school systems and taxpayers also benefit because local districts save $3,000 to $12,000 for each student that is educated outside the public school system. Accordingly, the states have tried to devise systems to aid church-supported schools, not by providing direct financial grants, but through providing textbooks, bus service, and other educational services. State legislatures argue that these services go to the children, not to the schools, and therefore do not violate the establishment clause. Very often the courts have agreed with this argument. For example, in *Board of Education v. Allen* (1968), the Supreme Court allowed a state program that loaned textbooks on secular topics to private and parochial school students. The divided Court upheld the practice, reasoning that the aid went to the students or to their parents rather than to the schools. The Court has also approved reimbursement of the costs of state-mandated standardized tests but has disapproved of providing free teaching materials other than textbooks.

However, in *Lemon v. Kurtzman* 403 U.S. 602 (1971), the Supreme Court prohibited salary supplements for lay teachers in parochial schools. The majority opinion, written by Chief Justice Warren Burger, was especially critical of the religious indoctrination in parochial schools, writing that "parochial schools involve substantial religious activity and purpose." The case also established a three-part test to see if a law offends the establishment clause (all three parts must be met): (1) the statute must have a secular purpose; (2) its primary effect must neither advance nor inhibit religion; and (3) it must avoid excessive governmental entanglement with religion. The *Lemon* test would be used by the Court for approximately 25 years and would also find its way into the Religious Freedom Restoration Act (declared unconstitutional by the Court in 1997). The Supreme Court has also held that a school district cannot provide instructional materials, such as maps, magazines, tape recorders and buses for field trips to parochial school students even though these are all used for secular, rather than religious, instruction. The Court held in *Wolman v. Walter* (1967) that the establishment clause was violated because of the "impossibility of separating the secular education function from the sectarian."

In *Everson v. Board of Education* 330 U.S. 1 (1947), the Supreme Court upheld a New Jersey subsidy of bus service to parochial schools. The provision of bus service was not a direct subsidy, but peripheral or incidental, similar to providing the school fire and police protection. The majority opinion focused on the fact that the aid went to the students or their parents, not directly to the school. The Court found no constitutional problem with "a general program to help parents get their children, regardless of their religion, safely and expeditiously to and from accredited schools." Accordingly, the wall of separation between church and state was not violated. In *Everson,* the Supreme Court for the first time ruled that the establishment clause of the First Amendment of the Constitution also applies to the states. Accordingly it applies to the actions of local school districts.

Justice Hugo Black believed that the Constitution's establishment clause demanded an absolute wall of separation between church and state. In *Everson,* Black explained his conception of the establishment clause, echoing Jefferson: "The first Amendment has erected a wall between church and state. That wall must be kept high and impregnable. We [the Supreme Court] could not approve the slightest breach." Surprisingly, Black's opinion held that there was no breach in the *Everson* case in which New Jersey had paid the bus fare of children riding public transit to parochial schools. Although Black would not countenance the "slightest breach" of the wall of separation, he reasoned that the reimbursement of the bus fare benefited the schoolchildren and their families rather than the parochial schools.

Initially the Court was hostile to state programs to provide services to parochial school students. The Supreme Court struck down a state plan to reimburse private and parochial schools for administering standardized achievement tests. The Court was troubled by the fact that the state could not guarantee that the funds would not be used for religious purposes and that the private schoolteachers would participate in preparing the tests (*Levitt v. Committee for Public Education*). Similarly, in *Meek v. Pittenger* (1975) the Supreme Court struck down state payment of auxiliary services such as the purchase of audiovisual equipment at parochial schools (curiously, this case involved the same law that was upheld in the 1968 *Board of Education v. Allen* case).

The results in these cases were not predictable and were

often fact-specific. For example, in *Wolman v. Walter* (1967), the Supreme Court upheld a program whereby public school employees provided both speech and hearing and psychological testing services for parochial school students at their schools. The Court reasoned that such services had no "educational content" and therefore the Court saw no threat to separation. Just two years earlier, in *Meek v. Pittenger,* the Court had struck down a similar program in part because the services were offered in a parochial school. In *Committee for Public Education v. Regan* (1980), the Supreme Court upheld a state-funded program in which the state reimbursed private and parochial schools for the cost of administering standardized tests. The private schools exercised no control over the tests themselves, which the Court felt prevented any forbidden entanglement between church and state.

In what has so far been the major case in this area, the Supreme Court, in *Aguilar v. Felton* (1985), struck down a program that used federal funds to pay the salaries of public school guidance counselors and teachers providing remedial and clinical help to low-income parochial school students. The Court held that the plan created an excessive government entanglement with religion and therefore failed the *Lemon* test. In Aguilar's companion case, *School District of Grand Rapids v. Ball* (1985), the Supreme Court struck down a school district's program that allowed public schoolteachers to teach secular classes in parochial school classrooms. The majority opinion held that the "symbolic union" of government and religion in one sectarian enterprise entangles the government with religion by implicitly endorsing the church that runs the school. Payment of the teachers' salaries was also seen as a direct subsidy to the parochial school.

In the decade following these cases the Reagan and Bush appointees to the Court adopted a more flexible stance that favored aid to church-supported schools. The Supreme Court found no establishment clause violation in *Zobrest v. Catalina Foothills School District* (1993), in which a California school district provided a sign language interpreter for a deaf student at a Catholic high school. The Court reasoned that there was no constitutional violation when the parochial school received only an "attenuated financial benefit" from the educational program that provided benefits neutrally without reference to the student's religious affiliation. It is interesting to compare this case with an earlier case such as *Wolman* (1977) in which the Court found payment for instructional materials in parochial schools to violate the establishment clause.

Finally, in 1997 the Supreme Court in *Agostini v. Felton* over-turned its 1985 ruling in *Aguilar v. Felton*. In the *Aguilar* case, a divided Supreme Court decided that remedial education funded by federal aid under Chapter 1 and performed by public school-teachers could not take place in parochial school buildings. The *Agostini* case held that the establishment clause did not prohibit public schoolteachers from giving remedial instruction in a parochial school. This was a major change in policy by the Supreme Court that had consistently held for over thirty years that public schoolteachers could not teach in parochial schools even when there was no religious instruction involved.

The U.S. Supreme Court, in *Board of Education of the Kiryas Joel Village School District v. Grumet* (1994), struck down New York state's creation of a special public school district to provide state-funded special education services for a community of Hasidic Jews. The community of approximately 8,500 members of the Satmae Hasidim sect of Orthodox Jews established a village based on their religious beliefs, including sexual segregation, a special dress code, and speaking Yiddish. In order to obtain state aid to the village's handicapped children, the state legislature allowed the village to establish a separate public school district that would only deal with the problems of the village's handicapped children. All children in the village attended private parochial schools except handicapped children who attended the public school, which provided services exclusively to the special needs children. The public school was staffed by secular teachers and had a purely secular curriculum. The Supreme Court held that this was a violation of the establishment clause. Because New York had created the school district along religious lines it violated the Constitution's requirement that government maintain its impartiality toward religion.

Proponents of state aid to children attending church-affiliated schools argue that the government should support the education of all schoolchildren, regardless of which school they select. They further argue that aid such as loaned textbooks, bus service, and special education services helps the children but not the schools. Opponents of such aid argue that the courts have merely used this to dodge the real issue. They argue that, pushed to its logical conclusion, there would be no limit on aid to church schools—including the payment of staff salaries—because the ultimate beneficiaries of the education are the students. Clearly the courts—and especially the current Supreme Court—are receptive to allowing state support of students who attend church-affiliated schools.

Several states have considered voucher systems that would give the parents of a child attending a private or church-affiliated school a voucher that would pay part or all of the student's tuition with public tax dollars. There appears to be substantial and diverse public support for voucher systems. Conservative Christians and Roman Catholics support voucher systems to gain government monies for their schools. Those who are opposed to or dissatisfied with the public schools also support vouchers. Some argue that the public school system would benefit by having competition from private schools. Additionally, some people would welcome vouchers that could potentially give poor schoolchildren the opportunity to escape their substandard neighborhood schools.

There are obvious constitutional problems. The Supreme Court has previously held, in *Committee v. Nyquist* (1973) and *Sloan v. Lemon* (1973), that reimbursement to church-affiliated schools—whether direct or indirect through tax credits—is unconstitutional. However, future Courts may be willing to rethink this issue. In *Mueller v. Allen* (1993), an evenly divided Supreme Court upheld a Minnesota law allowing parents of private and parochial school students to take a tax deduction for tuition and other educational expenses. The case is significant because the Court had struck down a similar law 20 years earlier in *Sloan v. Lemon*. The difference in the Minnesota law was that the deduction was also "available" to parents of public school students. The Court conveniently side-stepped the issue that parents of public school students do not actually pay tuition and thereby would not benefit in real terms. Nevertheless, Justice William Rehnquist, writing for the Court, found the tax scheme to be neutral. The fact that the bulk of the benefits would go to the parents of private and parochial school students was held to be irrelevant. The majority opinion stressed the value of supporting private schools not just for those students attending the schools but for the public in general. Rehnquist noted that the public benefited because each student educated in a private school reduced the taxpayer's burden of educating the student. Further, the private school system provided a standard for the public system and provided educational diversity.

In 1996 in *Simmons-Harris v. Goff*, an Ohio state court struck down the Ohio Pilot Scholarship Program that provided vouchers of up to $2,500 to Cleveland public school students to attend private or parochial schools. The court held that the voucher program violated the establishment clause because it would provide direct and substantial nonneutral government aid to sectarian schools. However, In June 1998 the Ohio Supreme Court reversed this ruling.

After the Wisconsin Supreme Court split on the issue of the validity of Milwaukee's voucher program in 1996, the case was sent back to the trial court. The trial court decided that the program was an unconstitutional violation of the church-state provisions of the Wisconsin state constitution. As this book went to press the case was on appeal to the Wisconsin Court of Appeals (*Jackson v. Benson; Thompson v. Jackson*).

Although the Supreme Court has struck down voucher systems in the past, those cases were decided long ago, and the present justices are far more receptive to aid to church-supported schools. Although early attempts at establishing voucher systems have run afoul of constitutional arguments, it may be possible for a state to design a system that could win judicial approval. An examination of past court cases reveals that the states have been able to draft legislation to give a good deal of aid to church-affiliated schools by targeting the aid to the students rather than to the schools. It is highly possible that a carefully drafted voucher system could win approval from the present Supreme Court.

Attempts to Amend the Constitution

Over the years, those who support organized prayer, Bible reading, and subjects with other religious content in the schools have sought to overturn the results of these court cases by amending the Constitution. Even if Congress would be willing to pass a law authorizing organized school prayer, such a law would probably be held unconstitutional by the Supreme Court. The Supreme Court often announces in its decisions that there are areas in the law that Congress should address. The Supreme Court has not invited Congress to pass laws to interpret the meaning of the First Amendment's religion clauses, however. It is clear that the Court feels that only the Court itself is equipped to interpret the scope of the First Amendment protections.

In our system of government there is a long tradition that Congress cannot change the Constitution on its own initiative or overturn a specific Supreme Court decision that it dislikes or that is unpopular with constituents. If members of Congress or citizens want the Constitution changed they must amend the Constitution itself. For example, the Twenty-sixth Amendment, ratified in 1971, gave 18-year-olds the right to vote.

Procedure for Amending the U.S. Constitution

Article V of the U.S. Constitution provides two mechanisms by which to make additions to the Constitution. The first method is the one usually employed. An amendment may be proposed in Congress, and if two-thirds of the members of both the House of Representatives and the Senate approve, the proposed amendment must then be ratified by the legislatures of three-quarters of the states.

There is a second method mentioned in the Constitution. A constitutional convention to add amendments can be convened at the request of the legislatures of two-thirds of the states. Proposed amendments can be ratified by a three-fourths vote of the convention. To date, no amendments have ever been added by a constitutional convention because none has ever been held. There is uncertainty about both the composition of such a convention and its operation, so it is unlikely to be an option.

History of Amendments

In fact, only 27 amendments have been made to the original 1789 document—a very small number considering the fact that the Constitution has been in effect for over 200 years and the country has obviously experienced many changes in that time.

During the late 1800s, members of Congress proposed no fewer than eleven different constitutional amendments dealing with church and state and religion in the schools. Generally, these amendments attempted to reduce the authority of the states in matters of religion. Although the existence of so many proposed amendments demonstrates that there was widespread interest, none of the proposed amendments has ever garnered the two-thirds majority needed. The most famous of these proposed amendments was the so-called Blaine Amendment, which was an early (1876) attempt to ban any state aid to church-supported schools, especially those run by the Catholic church. Although there was broad support for this amendment, it never received enough votes in Congress to be referred to the states for ratification. Interestingly, although the Blaine Amendment would have banned federal or state aid to church-supported schools and also prayer in public schools, it specifically stated that it did not prohibit Bible reading in the schools.

Recent Amendment Activity

After the 1962 and 1963 Supreme Court decisions in *Engel v. Vitale* and *Abington School District v. Schempp*, which many Americans viewed as shocking and out-of-step, there was a good deal of enthusiasm for a school prayer amendment, but the proposals never got the required two-thirds vote. In 1980, presidential candidate Ronald Reagan endorsed a school prayer amendment. Supporters of school prayer were buoyed by his endorsement but must have been disappointed when Reagan seemingly lost interest in the issue once elected. During the 1980s fundamentalist and conservative Christian organizations, particularly the Moral Majority and the Christian Coalition, assumed the lead in arguing for a school prayer amendment. Although none of the proposed amendments has been successful, enthusiasm for an amendment continues. In 1994 a proposed Religious Equality Amendment was introduced in Congress. At least two other amendments addressing religious expression were introduced in Congress in 1995.

Although a Democrat, Bill Clinton, was elected president in 1990, a Republican Congress was elected in 1992. The Republicans, led by Representative Newt Gingrich of Georgia, fashioned a "Contract with America," a program that emphasized a smaller government and a return to traditional American values. As part of its Contract with America, Newt Gingrich and the Republican leaders of Congress promised to introduce in Congress a school prayer amendment to the Constitution. Although a number of prominent Republican party leaders endorsed the idea of an amendment, no amendment was introduced until 1997. Written by Representative Ernest Istook of Oklahoma, the 1997 amendment not only would allow organized school prayer, but would also allow religious symbols, such as crosses, to be displayed in the schools and would allow tax dollars to be used to support private religious schools.

Resistance to Amendments

The primary resistance to proposed prayer amendments comes from two fronts. The first front is composed of individuals and groups such as Americans United for Separation of Church and State and People for the American Way who believe that the wall of separation established by the Supreme Court in the 1960s should be maintained. These individuals and groups are opposed to any change in the Constitution. Surprisingly, the other group resisting amendments comes from the religious right, because of disagreement about the focus that the amendment should take. Some think that the emphasis should be on restoring organized school prayer and daily Bible reading in the classroom while others want a much less specific amendment that would address any "discrimination" against religious speech and activity.

This squabbling among those associated with the religious right has prevented these groups from forming a consensus on any of the recently proposed religious amendments. The result has been that none of the proposed amendments has gathered significant support in Congress. For example, although numerous religious and politically conservative groups had called for a school prayer amendment, several prominent conservative groups withheld their support from the 1994 Religious Equality Amendment because they disagreed with the wording.

The situation became worse in 1995 when there were two competing amendments introduced. Although each amendment gathered supporters, no consensus emerged that would allow ether one to get a two-thirds vote of Congress. One amendment penned by Representative Ernest Istook, Jr., of Oklahoma focused on the school prayer issue and would have guaranteed organized student-sponsored school prayer in the public schools and allowed communities to decide if they could erect religious holiday displays including Christmas trees and crosses on Easter. The second amendment introduced in Congress by Representative Henry Hyde of Illinois had a broader focus and was aimed at prohibiting discrimination against religious speech and the protection of individuals who wanted to express such views in public. The net result of the squabble was to split support in Congress between the two amendments, which prevented both from gaining the necessary votes.

The scenario appears ready to repeat itself once again. Although the proposed 1997 Religious Freedom Amendment gained immediate support from a number of Christian groups including the Southern Baptist Convention and the National Association of Evangelicals, other groups held back. For example, the Christian Legal Society, a national association of evangelical lawyers who ordinarily support school prayer amendments, withheld their support from the amendment. The group pointed out that the actual language of the amendment uses the phrase "the people's right," which could be construed by the courts to mean that the rights could be enforced by Congress or state legislatures rather than individuals. This illustrates that although there may be broad support for some kind of constitutional amendment restoring organized prayer and other religious activity in the public schools, getting all the supporters to agree on the best approach may be far more difficult. History suggests that this can be difficult in practice since similar amendments have been proposed for over 100 years without success.

Looking Ahead

Religion in the schools promises to be a major political and cultural issue well into the next century. There is substantial disagreement in the United States about how these issues should be treated, and this disagreement promises to keep the area a controversial one. A not well-publicized but potentially far-reaching issue is the parental rights movement. If this movement catches on, it has the potential to completely change the present conception of the role of religion in the schools.

Another issue involves the Religious Freedom Restoration Act. This federal law, passed in 1993, provided, among other things, that federal, state, and local governments "shall not substantially burden a person's exercise of religion even if the burden results from a rule of general applicability ... except that Government may substantially burden a person's exercise of religion if it demonstrates that application of the burden to the person (1) is in furtherance of a compelling government interest; and (2) is the least restrictive means of furthering that compelling interest." The act is intended to deal with the free exercise of religion, not to the establishment of religion by the government. The act has been challenged on the grounds that it improperly attempts to impose on the courts a substantive rule.

In 1997, the U.S. Supreme Court, in *City of Boerne v. Flores,* overturned the 1993 Religious Freedom Restoration Act. Although involving a church that had a zoning dispute with a city, the case may have a major impact on the issue of religion in the schools. The Court ruled that the federal government is prohibited from passing a law that infringes on the practice of religion. By overturning the law, the Supreme Court opened the door to more regulation of religion by Congress. Opponents of the decision immediately vowed to rewrite the legislation and introduce it in the next session of Congress. A coalition of groups that often find themselves on opposing sides in religious issues, including many churches and organizations such as Americans United for Separation of Church and State, have come together to support a new version of the law that could survive the constitutional problems posed by the overturned law.

Another major issue involves the *Lemon* test used by the Supreme Court in religion cases. For many years the Supreme Court has used this measure, first applied in the 1971 case *Lemon v. Kurtzman,* in judging the legality of religious activities in the public schools. The Court may now have abandoned the test that had been used for 25 years to determine whether a practice in the schools violated the establishment clause. In *Lee v. Weisman,* the 1992 case striking down graduation prayers, neither the majority, concurring, or dissenting opinions applied the *Lemon* test when assessing the appropriateness of a religious invocation at a public school graduation ceremony. Although the Court did not announce that the test was no longer appropriate, the Court's complete silence led many commentators to suggest that it had been abandoned for all practical purposes. However, the 1997 cases from the Supreme Court have shown that the Court is still using— at least for now—the *Lemon* test. In the *Agostini v. Felton* decision, which overruled *Aguilar v. Felton,* the Court relied heavily on the test. The 1997 *Agostini* case permits state-funded remedial education in parochial schools. This case presented the perfect opportunity for the Court to jettison the test had it wanted to.

Two newer modes of analysis have emerged over the last few years, however. The first, suggested by Justice Kennedy's majority opinion in *Agostini,* involves "coercion." If the atmosphere surrounding the religious activity suggests that any student would be coerced into participating, then the state could be held to be proselytizing in violation of the establishment clause. The second mode of analysis, suggested by Justice Sandra Day O'Connor, involves the concept of the "endorsement" of a particular religious belief. Under this formulation, if the public school implicitly endorses the belief or practice, it will be held to be violating the establishment clause. Because both of these "tests" are by nature imprecise, they will be just as difficult to apply in practice as the three-part *Lemon* test. It might be fair to say that by 1992 the Supreme Court had adopted an ad hoc approach to cases involving religion into the schools that seemed to reflect the personal opinions of the individual justices rather than any systematic means of analyzing the issues.

Although there may be broad support for some kind of constitutional amendment restoring organized prayer and other religious activity in the public schools, getting all the supporters to agree on the best approach may be far more difficult. Because the issue is so emotional, it draws the interest of political leaders, sometimes out of conviction, sometimes out of opportunism. Since a substantial minority—or even a majority—of voters disagrees with many of the current approaches to this issue, a politician who promises change has the potential to build a strong base of support. Although both Presidents Reagan and Bush supported the concept of a school prayer amendment to the Constitution, it was never at the top of their political agendas and they never gave their full support to any movement favoring more religion in the schools. Bill Clinton, a moderate Democrat, has never endorsed a school prayer amendment. Clinton's education department did issue guidelines that take a moderate approach and allow some accommodation of religion in the schools while preserving the basic contours of our traditional church-state separation.

Future presidents will have the opportunity to affect this contentious area. But presidents may continue the policy of recent presidents in allowing the courts to control the content of religion in the schools. On the other hand, a president could be proactive by proposing legislation to Congress to promote religion in the schools. If the Supreme Court overturned such legislation, the president could then appeal to Congress and the state legislatures to support a constitutional amendment in the area. Additionally, future presidents will have the opportunity to shape the area through judicial appointments. There will be a number of vacancies to fill on the U.S. Supreme Court and other federal courts, and the beliefs and attitudes of these judges will play a large role in determining the law in this area.

Chronology 2

1620 Pilgrims settle at Plymouth Colony in what is now Massachusetts. Although the Pilgrims are motivated by strong religious beliefs, Plymouth Plantation is a curious blend of religious dissenters and nonreligious adventurers. The English financial backers of the colony are primarily interested in receiving a return on their investment. The dissenters—roughly half the population of the colony and including Miles Standish and John Alden—belong to a group of strict Protestants who dissent from the Anglican Church, the established church of England. The English dissenters—known as "separatists" and "Puritans"—object that, among other things, the teachings and practices of the Anglican church are too close to those of the Roman Catholic church. The separatists practice Congregationalism, which replaces church hierarchies by putting each local church congregation in control of its own affairs. These dissenting

1620 (cont)	sects are barely tolerated, and the Pilgrims leave England—first settling in Holland—to avoid persecution but also to set themselves up as a religious enclave that would serve as an example to their brethren back in England.
1630	The Puritans found Massachusetts Bay Colony, now Boston. Like the Pilgrims, they dissent from the doctrine and practices of the Anglican church. Although the Puritans fled England to escape religious persecution, they were not believers in religious toleration for others. The Bay Colony is a theocracy in which church and state are the same. Christians whose beliefs differ are not tolerated. Quakers are singled out for particularly harsh treatment.
1635	Roger Williams, exiled from the Massachusetts Bay Colony for his tolerance of other religions, founds Rhode Island, which offers religious freedom to all. Church and state are separate in Rhode Island from the start. Williams is perhaps the first person to use the phrase "wall of separation" when talking about the relationship of the government and religion.
1649	Maryland, founded by Lord Baltimore and a haven for Roman Catholics, passes the Act of Tolerance encouraging the free exercise of all Christian religions.
1689	The English Parliament passes the Act of Toleration, which allows Protestant dissenters—such as Puritans and separatists—to practice their religions. The act does not apply to either Jews or Roman Catholics, however. Parliament might have been influenced by John Locke's influential "Letters on Toleration," which appeared between 1689 and 1692.
1692	The colony of Massachusetts abolishes the official state church. However, each local government, except the city of Boston, is required to use tax monies to support all churches and clergy. Other New England states follow the practice.
1720	Start of twenty-year period of religious fervor called

the Great Awakening. The movement results in the fragmentation into several mainstream religious denominations. American Christianity becomes a diverse mixture of many small denominations. However, the established church in most colonies is still supported by tax revenues while the other churches generally receive no funds. There is no state-run system of public education, although most towns have schools that often are church-affiliated. Early school curriculums include both moral and religious instruction, including prayer and Bible reading.

1776   Publication of Thomas Paine's *Common Sense*. Paine's ideas, including a strong plea for the free exercise of religion, are later incorporated into the Bill of Rights. Paine argues that government should protect the individual right to practice religion. He also feels that there should be no established church and that the government should avoid active participation in religious subjects.

1782   The Virginia Bill for Establishing Religious Freedom is written by Thomas Jefferson, prohibiting penalties imposed on account of religious beliefs or practices and outlawing mandatory attendance or financial support of any religious activity. The bill is not immediately passed by the state legislature. There is substantial resistance to the proposal, especially the idea of withholding funds from an established church. Patrick Henry firmly believes that it is appropriate for the state of Virginia to use tax money to support teachers of the Christian faith. Henry represents the traditional view that the majority has the right to use tax money to support an established church. Jefferson and Madison, in contrast, consider that supporting an established church not only favors one church over another but also threatens the religious freedom of religious minorities.

1785   In his pamphlet "Memorial and Remonstrance against Religious Assessments," James Madison attacks a bill that would allow Virginia to financially support all churches. Madison points out that although the bill

1785 *(cont)*	proposes to use tax dollars to support all religions, it also has the potential to allow the state to favor one religion over another. Madison argues forcefully against any "establishment"—in other words an established church. This idea is later to find its way into the First Amendment. The Virginia proposal is defeated, and the next year Virginia passes Jefferson's Virginia Bill for Establishing Religious Freedom.
1791	The U.S. Constitution is ratified. The document is notable not only for what it includes but also what it excludes. Unlike all state constitutions, there is no reference to God or a Supreme Being and no provision for an established church or the furtherance of Christianity. Indeed, the First Amendment includes guarantees that "Congress shall make no law respecting an establishment of religion or prohibiting the free exercise thereof." The only other reference to religion in the document is found in Article VI, Clause 3, which prohibits "religious tests" for public office.
1833	Massachusetts—originally founded by the Pilgrims and Puritans—becomes the last state to give direct financial aid to churches. All other states cease such payments.
1840s	With immigration from Ireland and Germany, many eastern U.S. cities acquire a sizable population of Roman Catholics. The Catholic church establishes its own school systems, as well as colleges, in larger cities to help educate these immigrants and to combine religious and moral instruction in the curriculum. Instruction in the public schools includes both prayer and Bible reading. However, Catholics and other minorities recognize the instruction's strong Protestant influence. There is a backlash against both immigrants and the Roman Catholic church, both of which are viewed by many "nativist" Americans as pernicious foreign influences. The aptly named "Know Nothing" movement seeks to exclude foreign-born persons from elected office and to require a twenty-five-year waiting period for citizenship. The Native American party has nationwide support and

by 1854 controls state government in both Delaware and Massachusetts. Friction between Protestants and Catholics over public education remains a problem for the next one hundred years.

1868   Post–Civil War amendments added to the U.S. Constitution, including the Fourteenth Amendment, are enacted to protect legal rights of ex-slaves and other black Americans and to extend the reach of First Amendment rights of due process of law and equal protection before the law to the states.

1878   The Supreme Court, in *Reynolds v. U.S.*, banning the practice of polygamy, adopts the view that, although the free exercise clause of the Constitution protects individual religious beliefs, the Court could interfere with an action but not a belief. The Supreme Court does not completely reverse this view until 1963.

1892   In *Church of the Holy Trinity v. U.S.*, the Supreme Court states that "this is a Christian nation" and upholds a special exemption from immigration laws for the clergy.

1872   The Ohio Supreme Court bans in-class Bible reading in Cincinnati public schools in *Board of Education of Cincinnati v. Minor.*

1910   The Illinois Supreme Court bans in-class reading of the King James Bible in Chicago public schools in *People ex rel. Ring v. Board of Education of District 24.* Roman Catholics argue against the daily reading from the Protestant Bible in the public schools. The Court agrees that even if students are excluded from the Bible reading they are subjected to a religious stigma.

1923   Fundamentalist Christians, alarmed that the teaching of evolution may threaten their children's faith, lobby for state laws banning the teaching of evolution. Oklahoma passes the first such law.

During World War I, many states pass laws aimed at Germans or things Germanic. A parochial school

1923 *(cont)*	teacher at the Zion Parochial School in Nebraska is prosecuted under a Nebraska law prohibiting the teaching of German or any other foreign language to children not yet in high school for teaching German to ten-year-olds. The law is overturned by the U.S. Supreme Court in *Meyer v. Nebraska.*
1925	The world watches the Scopes trial, in which noted attorney Clarence Darrow represents high school biology teacher John Thomas Scopes, who is charged with violating a Tennessee law prohibiting the teaching of evolution in the public schools. Oregon voters, in response to the growing number of Catholics and Catholic schools in the state, pass a referendum that amends the state constitution to require all schoolchildren to attend public schools. Several private schools challenge the law. A unanimous Supreme Court, in *Pierce v. Society of Sisters,* holds that the Fourteenth Amendment protects the right to attend private schools and that, although the state of Oregon has the authority to regulate its public schools, it cannot require all students to attend only state-funded schools.
1928	Arkansas voters ban the teaching of evolution in the schools.
1940	Jehovah's Witnesses argue for their children to be excused from reciting the pledge of allegiance. Supreme Court Justice Felix Frankfurter writes for the Court in *Minersville School District v. Gobitis* that, despite the fact that religious precepts are violated, the government can require schoolchildren to recite the pledge of allegiance to create national unity. Frankfurter considers the recitation of the pledge a small price for the privilege of living in the United States. In *Cantwell v. Connecticut,* the Supreme Court for the first time rules that the free exercise clause of the First Amendment applies to the states and therefore to local school districts. Two Jehovah's Witnesses seek to pass out religious literature in downtown New

Haven, Connecticut, in violation of a law requiring a license to pass out religious literature.

1943   In *Virginia State Board of Education v. Barnette*, the Supreme Court invalidates a West Virginia law requiring mandatory recitals of the pledge of allegiance and flag salutes in public schoolrooms. In *Gobitis*, an almost identical case from three years earlier, the Court had upheld a similar law. There were three new members on the Court and two justices had changed their minds about the issue.

1947   In *Everson v. Board of Education*, the Supreme Court upholds a New Jersey subsidy of bus service to parochial schools, considering the provision of bus service not a direct subsidy but peripheral or incidental, similar to providing fire and police protection to schools. The majority opinion considers that the aid goes to the students or their parents, not directly to the school. In *Everson* the Supreme Court for the first time rules that the establishment clause of the First Amendment also applies to the states and therefore to the actions of local school districts.

1948   The Supreme Court hands down the first in a line of major cases that would change the contours of American society by largely eliminating religious activities in the public schools. The case, *People of Illinois ex rel. McCollum v. Board of Education*, bans use of public school buildings for release time religious instruction.

1952   In *Zorach v. Clauson*, the Supreme Court upholds a release time program taking place outside public school grounds. Earlier release time programs, in which religion classes were taught in public school classrooms, were struck down in 1948. In *Zorach*, that the school system assisted the programs by helping with registration and permitting the students to leave school did not seem important to the Court. Any entanglements were outweighed by the general benefits of the program.

1953   President Eisenhower nominates Governor Earl Warren of California to be the new Chief Justice of the

1953
(cont)
Supreme Court. A conservative Republican, once on the high court Warren proves to be a judicial activist and is especially eager to strike down laws that violate the separation of church and state, such as those allowing prayer in the public schools.

1954
Congress adds the words "under God" to the pledge of allegiance.

1956
President Eisenhower nominates William Brennan, a New Jersey jurist, to the Supreme Court. Brennan, a Catholic, proves to be a staunch defender of the separation of church and state.

1961
The Supreme Court, in *McGowan v. Maryland*, upholds Maryland's "blue law" mandating the closing of businesses on Sundays. Eight justices found no problem in Maryland's declaring the Christian sabbath as a day of rest for all citizens.

1962
Engel v. Vitale, one of the most important and far-reaching cases ever heard by the Supreme Court, rules unconstitutional a nondenominational school prayer written by the New York state Board of Regents. Justice Hugo Black writes for the Court that it is "no part of the business of government to compose official prayers."

1963
The Supreme Court hears another major school prayer case, *Abington School District v. Schempp*, and again rules that school-organized prayer is unconstitutional, going even further than *Engel* in also banning the recitation of the Lord's Prayer and Bible reading in public schools. Opposition to the banning of school prayer is swift, from politicians, from the pulpit, and from groups, such as the right-wing John Birch Society.

The Court recognizes that the free exercise clause protects both religious actions as well as religiously motivated actions, holding that unemployment benefits cannot be denied to a Seventh Day Adventist who refuses to work on Saturdays.

The Creation Research Society is founded by fundamentalist Christians to combat the teaching of evolution in the public schools.

1965   With the Vietnam War escalating, more individuals wish to resist the selective service's military draft. In *United States v. Seegher*, the Supreme Court allows conscientious objectors—those opposed to war—to avoid military service if their objection is based on "religious training and belief." There is no requirement that they belong to a sect that itself is opposed to war.

1967   In *Wolman v. Walter*, the Supreme Court holds that a school district cannot provide instructional materials such as maps, magazines, tape recorders, and buses for field trips to parochial school students, even though they would be used for secular, rather than religious, purposes. The Court holds that the establishment clause would be violated because of the "impossibility of separating the secular education function from the sectarian."

1968   In *Board of Education of Central School Dist. No. 1 v. Allen*, the Supreme Court upholds the loan of textbooks to a parochial school, on the grounds that the books aid the students rather than the school.

In *Epperson v. Arkansas*, the Supreme Court, in a unanimous opinion, strikes down an Arkansas statute that prohibits the teaching of evolution. The Court points out that the ban was enacted entirely to "aid, foster, or promote" one religion over another and thereby offends the establishment clause of the First Amendment.

1970   Court upholds state tax exemptions for property and income of religious institutions based on historical practices in *Walz v. Tax Commission of New York*.

1971   In *Lemon v. Kurtzman*, the Supreme Court prohibits salary supplements for lay teachers in parochial schools. In the majority opinion, Chief Justice Warren

1971
(cont)
Burger writes that "parochial schools involve substantial religious activity and purpose." The case also establishes a three-part test to see if a law violates the establishment clause known as the *Lemon* test.

1972
The Court upholds the right of Amish parents to withhold their children from public school, despite the state of Wisconsin's compulsory schooling law, in *Yoder v. Wisconsin*. Although the state has a strong interest in requiring children to attend school, it does not overbalance the burden on religious freedom of compelling them to attend school.

1973
The Supreme Court prohibits tax credits and grants to parents of parochial school students in *Committee for Public Education and Religious Liberty v. Nyquist* and *Sloan v. Lemon*.

The Court strikes down a state plan to reimburse private and parochial schools for administering standardized achievement tests in *Levitt v. Committee for Public Education*.

In Texas, where all school districts adopt textbooks recommended by the state, Mel and Norma Gabler found Educational Research Analysts to lobby the state to not adopt textbooks that undermine Judeo-Christian values and American pride.

1975
In *Meek v. Pittenger*, the Supreme Court strikes down state payment for auxiliary services such as the purchase of audiovisual equipment at parochial schools. Curiously, this case involved the same law that was upheld in the 1968 *Allen* case.

1976
In a 5-to-4 decision, the Supreme Court upholds Maryland's program to provide grants to private colleges, including church-supported colleges, ruling that this program does not violate the establishment clause even though the aid goes to religious organizations (*Roemer v. Board of Public Works*).

1977
The Supreme Court approves a program whereby

public school employees provide both speech and hearing and psychological testing services for parochial school students at their schools, reasoning that such services have no "educational content" and that the Court sees no possibility of proselytizing (*Wolman v. Walter*).

1978   The IRS threatens to withdraw tax exemptions from private and parochial schools that are established to avoid court-ordered desegregation.

1980   In *Stone v. Graham,* the Supreme Court bans the posting of the Ten Commandments in public schools even when financed with private funds, ruling that the purpose is religious and therefore prohibited by the establishment clause.

In *Committee for Public Education v. Regan,* the Supreme Court upholds a state-funded program in which the state reimburses private and parochial schools for the cost of administering standardized tests. The private schools exercised no control over the tests themselves, which the Court rules prevents any forbidden entanglement between church and state.

1981   The California Supreme Court, in *California Teachers Ass'n v. Riles*, rules that "lending" public schools to parochial schools is contrary to the California state constitution, although the Supreme Court has held the practice to be not contrary to the U.S. Constitution.

A state university cannot deny use of its facilities to a religious club, the Supreme Court, in *Widmar v. Vincent,* rules. It would be a violation of the students' First Amendment rights and would put the university in the position of excluding groups that the university deemed religious, while granting use to groups that it perceived as not religious. The equal access language in this case led to legislative action in 1984.

The Louisiana legislature passes the Balanced Treatment for Creation-Science and Evolution-Science in Public School Instruction Act that mandates that any

1981
(cont)
school teaching evolution must also provide equal classroom time to the teaching of creation-science, based on the biblical account of creation. Although applauded by religious leaders, the law is immediately challenged.

1982
President Reagan becomes the first president to endorse an amendment allowing prayer in the public schools. Reagan tells Congress that it is time to "allow prayer back in our schools."

1983
In *Mueller v. Allen*, a closely divided Supreme Court holds that a Minnesota law allowing parents of private and parochial school students to take a tax deduction for tuition and other educational expenses is constitutional. The case is significant because the Court had earlier struck down a similar law. What saved the Minnesota law was that the deduction was also "available" to parents of public school students. The Court conveniently side-stepped the issue that parents of public school students do not actually pay tuition and thereby would not benefit in real terms.

The Supreme Court upholds the IRS's disallowance of nonprofit, tax-free status to private schools that discriminate against students or prospective students on the basis of race in *Bob Jones University v. U.S.*

The school prayer amendment, supported by President Reagan and Senate leaders, passes the Senate by a vote of 56 to 44. Because it lacks the constitutionally required two-thirds vote, the measure fails.

1984
Congress passes the federal Equal Access Act, which prohibits discrimination against student groups on the basis of religious, political, or philosophical views, ruling that if a public school allows other "non-curriculum related groups" such as clubs to use its facilities, then the school must give equal access to religious groups.

The Republican party platform vows to allow school prayer, by constitutional amendment if necessary.

In *Lynch v. Donnelly*, the Court posits that the so-called wall of separation is "not a wholly accurate description of the practical aspects of the relationship that in fact exists between church and state because the Constitution affirmatively mandates accommodation, not merely tolerance, of all religions and forbids hostility towards any."

1985   The Supreme Court, in *Wallace v. Jaffree*, invalidates an Alabama law allowing a one-minute period of silence at the start of each school day "for meditation or voluntary prayer." A divided court (6 to 3) concludes that this mandated moment of silence amounts to "the State's endorsement of prayer activity" that transgresses the proper wall of separation between church and state. Merely allowing students to be excused is held insufficient.

In *Aguilar v. Felton*, the Supreme Court strikes down a program that uses federal funds to pay the salaries of public school guidance counselors and teachers providing remedial and clinical help to low-income parochial school students. The Court holds that the plan creates an excessive government entanglement with religion and therefore fails the *Lemon* test.

In *School District of Grand Rapids v. Ball*, the Supreme Court rules unconstitutional a school district's program that allows public schoolteachers to teach secular classes in parochial school classrooms, holding that the "symbolic union" of government and religion in one sectarian enterprise entangles the government with religion by implicitly endorsing the church that runs the school.

1986   Louisiana passes the Balanced Treatment Act requiring equal time for the teaching of "creation science" whenever the theory of evolution is taught in school science classes. A few states have enacted such laws; others have rejected such measures.

1987   In *Edwards v. Aguillard*, the Supreme Court invalidates Louisiana's Balanced Treatment Act, a law requiring

1987 *(cont)*	public schools to provide equal time for the teaching of evolution and creation science. Two justices dissented and would have allowed Louisiana to mandate the teaching of "creation science" as an alternative to the theory of evolution.
1988	President Ronald Reagan appoints Anthony Kennedy to replace Lewis Powell on the Supreme Court. His conservative reputation causes surprise to many, including Reagan, when he sides with the majority in striking down a Texas law outlawing the burning of the American flag. In 1992 Kennedy writes the majority opinion in *Lee v. Wiseman*, striking down religious invocations at high school graduation ceremonies.
1989	A federal district court prohibits a local Massachusetts school district from renting space in a Roman Catholic parish center for classroom use. In *Spacco v. Bridgewater School Department*, the court holds that the use of church property has the effect of endorsing the particular religion.
1990	Using the *Lemon* test, the Supreme Court, in *Board of Education of the Westside Community Schools v. Mergens*, upholds the constitutionality of the federal Equal Access Act, enacted to give equal access to public school facilities for religious groups and clubs. The Court holds that, although there is some involvement of school officials in the appealed case, this does not constitute entanglement with religion nor an endorsement of any particular religion.
	The Supreme Court, in *Employment Division v. Smith*, holds that religious belief does not excuse commission of a crime (specifically, in the case, the use of peyote by Native Americans). Alarmed by the consequences for other religious practices, such as receiving sacramental wine at communion services, religious groups ask Congress for additional protections. Congress responds in 1993 by passing the Religious Freedom Restoration Act.
1991	President George Bush appoints Clarence Thomas to

the Supreme Court to replace Thurgood Marshall. Although both are African American, Bush denies that race is a factor. Philosophically, Thomas is a conservative and almost the complete opposite of Marshall, the most liberal member of the Court.

1992   A divided Supreme Court, in *Lee v. Weisman*, rules that an invocation at a public school graduation ceremony in Providence, Rhode Island, violates the establishment clause. Justice Kennedy, writing for the majority, argues that the public atmosphere constitutes coercion on students. Justice Scalia dissents, writing that the majority opinion "lay[s] waste" to traditional nonsectarian prayers at public events and that the majority's use of "coercion" is a "bulldozer of its social engineering." With *Lee v. Weisman*, the Court may have abandoned the *Lemon* test that had been used for twenty-five years to determine whether a practice in the schools violated the establishment clause.

1993   Congress passes the Religious Freedom Restoration Act. The act provides, among other things, that federal, state, and local governments "shall not substantially burden a person's exercise of religion even if the burden results from a rule of general applicability—except that Government may substantially burden a person's exercise of religion—if it demonstrates that application of the burden to the person (1) is in furtherance of a compelling government interest; and (2) is the least restrictive means of furthering that compelling interest." The act is intended to deal with the free exercise of religion, not the establishment of religion by the government. The act has been challenged on the grounds that it improperly attempts to impose on the courts a substantive rule.

The Supreme Court finds no establishment clause violation in *Zobrest v. Catalina Foothills School District*, in which a California school district provided a sign language interpreter for a deaf student at a Catholic high school. The Court rules that there is no constitutional violation when the parochial school receives only an

1993
(cont)

"attenuated financial benefit" from the educational program that provides benefits neutrally without reference to the student's religious affiliation.

In *Lamb's Chapel v. Center Moriches School District*, the Supreme Court holds that a school district cannot deny access to school facilities to a church group that wants to show a film on child rearing, although the film was only shown to the church group and after school hours.

Distribution of Bibles by the Gideons in public schools is struck down as a violation of the establishment clause in *Berger v. Rensselaer Central School Corp.*

1994

The Supreme Court, in *Board of Education of the Kiryas Joel Village School District v. Grumet*, strikes down New York state's creation of a special public school district to provide state-funded special education services to a community of Hasidic Jews.

Georgia enacts a "moment of quiet reflection" for public schoolteachers to begin the school day. Although the practice is immediately attacked as a "silent prayer," the silent moment is upheld in *Bowen v. Gwinnett School District* because the law specifically disclaims any religious purpose. Accordingly, the federal district court holds that the law does not violate the Constitution.

Mississippi enacts a law allowing student-initiated voluntary prayer at all assemblies, sporting events, commencement exercises, and other school-related events. The law is immediately challenged by the ACLU, and a Mississippi federal district judge, in *Ingebretsem v. Jackson Public School District*, upholds the section of the law allowing prayers at commencement exercises but strikes down the parts of the act allowing prayer at assemblies and other school-related events.

An Idaho school district allows student leaders to say a prayer at graduation if a majority of the graduating seniors agree. A federal court of appeals, in *Harris v. Joint School District No. 241*, rules that the compulsory nature of graduation makes the graduation prayer improper and that school officials cannot sidestep their responsibilities by delegating the decision to the students.

In *Guyer v. School Board of Alahua County*, a federal court in Florida refuses to order a school district to remove Halloween decorations after a parent complains that Halloween is a pagan religious holiday. The judge rules that Halloween is a secular and cultural holiday and allows the decorations to stay.

1995   The U.S. Department of Education issues guidelines on religious activity in public schools. The guidelines allow student prayer and Bible reading by individuals or groups that is not disruptive. The wearing of religious clothing or symbols is permitted, as is limited proselytizing and the distribution of religious literature. Prohibited activities include prayer that is endorsed by a teacher or other school authorities. Teachers may teach about religion but may not advocate a particular religion and may not encourage either religious or antireligious activity.

The Supreme Court issues a preliminary injunction against Wisconsin's voucher plan for religious schools. Under the state plan, the state would pay the tuition for low-income children in both private non-sectarian schools and parochial schools. The injunction does not affect vouchers to be used in the nonsectarian schools.

The Christian Coalition, headed by Ralph Reed, issues its "Contract with the American Family." One of the ten proposals calls for school vouchers.

The Supreme Court, in *Rosenberger v. Rector & Visitors of University of Virginia*, holds that a state university that uses student funds to support other campus clubs and organizations cannot withhold funds from a religious group to publish a Christian magazine.

1995
(cont)

The Court reasons that this is improper viewpoint discrimination. At this time it is unclear how much influence this case will have on the public schools.

1996

A Texas student objects to her team policy of praying before and after games and at practices and pep rallies with the encouragement of coaches and the choir's singing of religious hymns. The prayers at pep rallies stop, but the other practices continue, and she files suit in federal court. In *Doe v. Duncanville Independent School District*, the courts order the in-school prayers to stop but rule that the singing of traditional choral music is not an endorsement of religion even when the music is based on sacred themes.

A federal court in Illinois holds that the state's policy of closing the public schools on Good Friday violates the Constitution. Interestingly, the court notes that both Christmas and Thanksgiving have lost their religious significance for many Americans and that school closings on those days had a secular and not religious purpose.

The Wisconsin state legislature expands Milwaukee's voucher program to include private and parochial schools. Parents of school-age children in the city can use the government vouchers to pay for tuition in such schools. The practice is challenged and the program is put on hold.

The movement grows to add a parental rights amendment to each state constitution and eventually to the U.S. Constitution as well. The amendment would forbid the government—including the public schools—from interfering with or usurping the right of a parent to direct the upbringing of the child. The amendment would make it easier for parents to challenge classroom materials that they find objectionable. Some argue that the amendment would compel the government to pay tuition for parents who want their children educated in church-affiliated schools.

1997

Alabama legislators debate a proposal to seek voter

approval for a state constitutional amendment that would require all public schools to set aside time to read prayers from the Congressional Record and to discuss topics such as the historical significance of the Ten Commandments.

The Supreme Court, revisiting a case it decided in 1994, again strikes down the creation of a special public school district at Kiryas Joel, New York, to provide state-funded special education services for a community of Hasidic Jews. The Court holds that the new state statute allowing the district still offends the establishment clause.

Ohio state court strikes down the Ohio Pilot Scholarship Program that provides vouchers of up to $2,500 to Cleveland public school students to attend private or parochial schools. The state court, in *Simmons-Harris v. Goff*, holds that the voucher program violates the establishment clause because it provides direct and substantial nonneutral government aid to sectarian schools.

After the Wisconsin Supreme Court split on the issue of the validity of Milwaukee's voucher program in 1996, the case was sent back to the trial court. The trial court decided that the program was an unconstitutional violation of the church-state provisions of the Wisconsin state constitution. The case is currently on appeal to the Wisconsin Court of Appeals (*Jackson v. Benson; Thompson v. Jackson*).

The Supreme Court, in *Agostini v. Felton*, overturns its 1985 decision in *Aguilar v. Felton*, that remedial education funded by federal aid under Chapter 1 could not take place in parochial school buildings. The 1997 case holds that the establishment clause does not prohibit public schoolteachers from giving remedial instruction in a parochial school. This is a major change by the Supreme Court that had uniformly held for over thirty years that public schoolteachers could not teach in parochial schools even when there was no religious instruction involved.

1997
(cont)

The Supreme Court, in *City of Boerne v. Flores,* overturns the 1993 Religious Freedom Restoration Act. Although the case involves a church that has a zoning dispute with a city, the case may have a major impact on the issue of religion in the schools. According to the overturned federal statute, the federal government is prohibited from passing a law that infringes on the practice of religion. By overturning the law the Supreme Court opens the door to more regulation of religion by Congress. Opponents of the decision immediately vow to rewrite the legislation and introduce it in the next session of Congress.

1998

Wisconsin Supreme Court upholds Milwaukee's voucher program.

Biographical Sketches 3

Jim Bakker (1939–)

A former associate of Pat Robertson at the Christian Broadcasting Network, Jim Bakker became a household name when he was charged with misusing funds from his ministry. Together with his wife, Tammy Fae Bakker, Jim Bakker founded PTL ("Praise the Lord" or "People That Love"), which combined television evangelism with a religious theme park. PTL also called for a conservative social and political agenda, including the return of religion to the public schools. Bakker and his wife were investigated by the federal government for abusing their tax-exempt ministry for private gain. The resulting bankruptcy of PTL and the public conviction and incarceration of Bakker created a very negative image for all televangelists and eroded much of their financial and political support. This loss of support ended up derailing efforts to press Congress to pass a constitutional amendment to allow prayer in the public schools.

Hugo L. Black (1886–1971)

A one-time small-town Ku Klux Klan member, Hugo L. Black rose to serve on the U.S. Supreme Court and came to write one of the most enduring court opinions protecting separation of church and state. Black grew up in rural Alabama and graduated from Birmingham Medical College but gave up medicine to enroll at the University of Alabama Law School. He became a lawyer in private practice and later a local judge and rose to national prominence when he won an upset election as U.S. senator from Alabama. In Washington he became a loyal and vocal supporter of the Roosevelt New Deal.

Black was appointed to the Supreme Court in 1937 by Roosevelt and served with distinction until 1971. The nomination was highly controversial because of Black's former membership in the Ku Klux Klan. But he surprised many of his critics by becoming a strong supporter of both civil rights and freedom of religion once on the Court. Black enjoyed a long tenure on the Court and was an important member of the famous Warren Court that handed down many liberal opinions during the 1950s and early 1960s.

Black is perhaps best remembered for writing many of the era's important decisions, most notably *Gideon v. Wainwright* (1963), which requires that defendants in criminal cases be represented by counsel, and *Engel v. Vitale* (1962), which banned prayer in public schools. The highly controversial school prayer case thrust both the Court and Black into the limelight. He was vilified in many quarters, especially by many Christians who believed that the Court, and Black in particular, had gone far beyond the intent of the nation's founders.

Black believed that the establishment clause demanded an absolute wall of separation between church and state. In *Everson v. Board of Education* (1947), Black explained his conception of the establishment clause, echoing Jefferson's earlier view: "The first Amendment has erected a wall between church and state. That wall must be kept high and impregnable. We [Supreme Court] could not approve the slightest breach."

William J. Brennan, Jr. (1906–1997)

The son of Irish immigrants, William J. Brennan graduated with distinction from the University of Pennsylvania and Harvard Law School. Before and after service in World War II, Brennan was a labor lawyer in private practice in Newark, New Jersey. After serving on New Jersey's Superior Court and Supreme Court, he was appointed to the U.S. Supreme Court by Eisenhower. Brennan proved to be a strong advocate of civil rights and freedom of religion during his term from 1956 to 1990. A member of the Warren Court, Brennan became the leader of the Supreme Court's liberal minority after 1970, and his ability to build consensus preserved and even extended the liberal decisions of the Court, even after the appointment of a number of avowed conservatives.

Brennan was a staunch upholder of separation of church and state and often found himself in the minority. By the mid-1970s he was the only justice who consistently voted against all aid to religious schools, including the loaning of textbooks.

William Jennings Bryan (1860–1925)

Bryan was an unsuccessful Democratic presidential candidate in 1896, 1902, and 1908. A renowned orator, Bryan gained a national reputation and the Democratic nomination in 1896 after making his famous "Cross of Gold" speech, aimed at the gold standard. After his three unsuccessful presidential campaigns, he became Woodrow Wilson's secretary of state. Bryan tried to keep America on a pacifist course in foreign policy. He eventually resigned after he broke with Wilson over U.S. involvement in World War I.

Bryan was a fundamentalist who believed in the literal truth of the biblical account of creation. After his retirement from politics he often delivered lectures on the religious circuit. He was strongly opposed to the teaching of evolution in the schools and believed that it was up to the citizens to decide whether the teachings of Darwin belonged in the school curriculum.

Today Bryan is best remembered for his defense of Tennessee's antievolution law in the famous 1925 Scopes trial. The statute banned the teaching of evolution in any school or college in the state. Fundamentalists recruited Bryan, one of the most recognizable figures of his day, to argue the state's case, hoping to draw national attention to the issue. Bryan won and Scopes was convicted. Bryan died just a week after the end of the trial.

Warren Burger (1907–1995)

Chief Justice of the Supreme Court from 1969 to 1986, Warren Burger, the son of immigrant parents, worked his way through both the University of Minnesota and Mitchell College of Law (at the time St. Paul College of Law). Following two decades of private practice, Burger, an active Republican, was appointed assistant attorney general in charge of the civil division of the Justice Department. Burger was appointed a judge of the U.S. Court of

Appeals for the District of Columbia and was nominated by President Nixon to be chief justice of the Supreme Court upon the retirement of Earl Warren.

Unlike Warren, Burger was known as a strict constructionist, and the Burger Court proved more conservative than the Warren Court. However, by today's standards the Court was judicially active during Burger's tenure as chief justice and delivered several controversial opinions, especially in the area of religion and the schools. Although known as a conservative, Burger himself wrote one of the most controversial opinions in the area, *Lemon v. Kurtzman* (1971), which took a strong stand that any entanglement between church and state would not be tolerated in the schools. Burger, writing for the Court, held that state salary supplements or aid for secular instruction in parochial schools offended both the establishment clause and the free exercise clause: "Government is to be entirely excluded from the area of religious instruction and churches excluded from the affairs of government."

He also wrote the majority opinion in *Wisconsin v. Yoder* (1972), an 8-to-1 decision in which the Court upheld the right of Amish parents to withhold their children from public school despite the state of Wisconsin's compulsory schooling law. Burger also served as head of the U.S. Bicentennial Commission.

Clarence Darrow (1857–1938)

Noted criminal attorney who defended John Scopes, Darrow was perhaps the best-known trial attorney of his day, defending mobsters, businessmen, and Eugene Debs, the socialist labor leader. Darrow volunteered to help the ACLU defend the Tennessee teacher, who agreed to challenge the state's law prohibiting the teaching of the theory of evolution.

William O. Douglas (1898–1980)

Serving as an associate justice of the Supreme Court from 1939 to 1975, Douglas holds the record for longevity on the high court. Although perhaps best remembered for his reputation as a supporter of the environment, Douglas was also a Bill of Rights expert and penned many notable opinions involving religion in the schools. Born in Maine, Minnesota, and educated at the University of Washington, Douglas taught at Yale Law School. He was selected by President Roosevelt to serve as chairman of the newly created Securities and Exchange Commission in 1937 and was appointed to the Supreme Court just two years later. Because of his background in securities regulation, Douglas was often called upon to write the Court's opinions concerning business matters. However, his lasting legacy is in the area of civil liberties, especially those guaranteed by the First Amendment. His book, *A Living Bill of Rights* (1961), deals with civil liberties.

Although known as a liberal, Douglas was a vocal supporter of religious rights. His views seem very close to those held by Hugo Black, who was the staunchest supporter of absolute separation of church and state. Although Douglas had voted with the majority in *Everson v. Board of Education* (1947) to allow governments to pay for bus transportation for parochial school children, two decades later in *Board of Education v. Allen* (1968) he voted against taxpayer financial support for textbooks. He viewed bus transportation as neutral; allowing the parochial schools to select books to be paid for with tax dollars was too much of an entanglement under the First Amendment. Douglas was also the lone dissenter in *Wisconsin v. Yoder,* which allowed Old Amish believers to avoid high school on religious grounds. Douglas dissented on the grounds that the majority's focus was on the parental right to withhold education, but that the proper focus should be on the child's right to obtain an education. However, he thought the action of withholding children from school was beyond the bounds of the free exercise clause of the First Amendment.

Jerry Falwell (1932–)

Pastor of the Thomas Road congregation in suburban Virginia, Jerry Falwell became a national figure in the 1980s with his leadership of the Moral Majority advocacy group. Although Falwell was well known among conservative Christians, his influence increased with the success of his radio and television show, "The Old Time Gospel Hour," which reached millions.

He established the Moral Majority in 1979 (later renamed the Liberty Federation) to put conservative Christian views into the political arena, advocating a nationwide return to "family values" that would better represent the needs and desires of what he termed the "moral majority" of Americans. Along with the limitation of equal rights for women and gays, the Moral Majority advocated a return of Christianity to the classroom. Both Falwell and his organization were strong supporters of returning prayer to the classroom. By 1989 Falwell scaled back his national presence as he encountered financial problems and faced charges from the IRS about the tax-exempt status of the organization.

Abe Fortas (1910–1982)

Abe Fortas, an associate justice of the U.S. Supreme Court from 1965 to 1969, is best remembered as President Johnson's unsuccessful choice to succeed Earl Warren as chief justice. Fortas was forced to resign from the Court after it was disclosed that he had a financial relationship with a former client who was under federal investigation. He returned to private law practice and died in 1982. Fortas wrote the Supreme Court's majority opinion in *Epperson v. Arkansas* (1968), which overturned an Arkansas law prohibiting the teaching of evolution in the state's schools and universities.

Fortas wrote that the Arkansas law favored the biblical account of creation and thus unconstitutionally breached Jefferson's wall of separation. It is interesting to speculate how the Supreme Court's decisions would have evolved had Fortas become chief justice. President Nixon appointed the conservative Warren Burger as chief justice. The Burger Court was called upon to decide a number of important issues involving religion and the schools.

Felix Frankfurter (1882–1965)

Felix Frankfurter, born in Austria, was raised in poverty in New York City's Lower Eastside. He attended City University and later Harvard Law School. After brief stints in private practice and government service, he taught at Harvard Law School for twenty-five years.

He was an active Zionist and also was involved in the defense of Sacco and Vanzetti and the founding of the American Civil Liberties Union. He was a close adviser to President Roosevelt, who appointed him to the Supreme Court in 1939 to replace Justice Benjamin Cardozo. He served on the Court until 1962. He usually supported New Deal legislation. In later years he generally favored the doctrine of judicial restraint, which holds that the courts should not substitute their views for those of the elected legislatures.

Frankfurter was one of the true legal scholars on the Court and was called upon to write the Court's opinions in some of the most politically charged cases on the separation of church and state. Frankfurter wrote the opinion in *Minersville School District v. Gobitis* (1940) in which Jehovah's Witnesses asked to be excused from saying the pledge of allegiance. Frankfurter, writing for the Court, held that, despite the fact that their religious precepts prohibited reciting the pledge, the government could force school-children to recite the pledge of allegiance to create national unity.

Mel Gabler (1915–)

A conservative Christian from Longview, Texas, Gabler has had an enormous influence on textbook selection and textbook publishing nationwide. A former Sunday school teacher and PTA president, Gabler first got involved in textbook issues in 1961 when he objected to his son's high school history book. In 1973 Gabler and his wife, Norma, established the Educational Research Analysts organization, which studies school textbooks and other classroom resources for material that the Gablers consider anti-Christian or antifamily. The state of Texas adopts a statewide list of approved textbooks that can be adopted by local school districts. Because few individuals were interested in the textbook adoption process, the Gablers were able to exert a strong influence over the state's selection of textbooks. Because publishers didn't want to lose the massive Texas market, they edited their textbooks to avoid offending the Gablers.

Like Tim LaHaye, the Gablers view "secular humanism" as the enemy of Christianity and see a conspiracy in the deletion of Christian teachings from school textbooks. They object to biology texts that promote evolution over the biblical account of creation. They also view sex education and drug education as counter to scripture. The Gablers have shared their techniques with other conservative Christians nationwide. In many cases these individuals or groups have been able to influence textbook adoption decisions made by individual school boards.

Thomas Jefferson (1743–1826)

The primary author of the Declaration of Independence, the nation's first secretary of state under George Washington, and John Adam's vice president, Jefferson served as the third president of the United States from 1801 to 1809. A staunch defender of the separation of church and state, Jefferson remains one of the two or three most important influences on the course of religion in the schools of the United States. Although called an atheist, Jefferson was really a deist who believed in God and worshiped regularly. However, even before the American Revolution, Jefferson developed strongly held views on the need for an absolute separation of church and state. In his Virginia Bill for Establishing Religious Freedom, he sought to grant religious freedom and equality. At the time, this was a radical proposition and it did not initially pass. Only years later, with James Madison's help, was it approved by the Virginia Assembly.

Jefferson was one of the first influential thinkers to argue that religious freedom required the separation of church and state. His famous phrase, the "wall of separation," is still used today to describe the barrier erected in public life between the spiritual and the secular worlds. Although Jefferson probably did think that the states could have some involvement in religious matters, he evidently believed that the federal government should have no involvement with religion and could be termed an "absolute" separationist. Unlike his predecessors in the presidency, George Washington and John Adams, Jefferson did not proclaim a national day of thanksgiving, which he would have regarded as a religious exercise. Even James Madison returned to the yearly proclamations when he became president after Jefferson.

It is clear that Jefferson himself regarded as one of his most important, lasting contributions his establishing of religious freedom. He designed his own tombstone and its inscription, which lists what he thought were his greatest accomplishments. Interestingly, his service as president is not mentioned. The inscription reads: "Thomas Jefferson—author of the Declaration of American Independence, of the Statute of Virginia for Religious Freedom, and Father of the University of Virginia."

Anthony M. Kennedy (1936–)

A native of California and graduate of Stanford University, the London School of Economics, and Harvard Law School, Anthony Kennedy was appointed to the Supreme Court by President Reagan in 1989. He had spent several years in private practice and as a justice of the U.S. Court of Appeals for the Ninth Circuit.

Although Kennedy was predicted to be conservative, he surprised many, including Reagan, by siding with the liberal justices in overturning a Texas statute outlawing the desecration of the American flag on First Amendment grounds. Kennedy, a Catholic, wrote some of the most important recent opinions on the separation of church and state, including the majority opinion in *Lee v. Weisman* (1992), which forbids school-sponsored prayers at public school graduation ceremonies.

Beverly LaHaye (1930–) and
Tim LaHaye (1926–)

The LaHayes are influential proponents of religion and prayer in the public schools. Tim LaHaye, an ordained minister, was a co-founder with Jerry Falwell of the Moral Majority and his own American Coalition for Traditional Values. He has been influential in promoting the conservative Christian agenda in national politics. LaHaye has been successful in getting many Christians involved in the political process and making the Republican party responsive to their concerns.

The LaHayes, who had for several years conducted marriage seminars for Christians in San Diego, first gained national prominence after the publication of their book *The Act of Marriage: The Beauty of Sexual Love.* This sex manual became a bestseller with born-again Christians. Tim LaHaye also gained prominence in education with his books. *The Battle for the Mind* (1980) and *The Battle for the Public Schools* (1983) pointed to "secular humanism" as a threat to traditional American values. The books criticize current school textbooks as not really "neutral" in their treatment of religion but as presenting a godless view of the world and for what he sees as a relativistic approach to morals, which, he argues, fails to teach students about right and wrong. These books have been instrumental in motivating Christians to challenge textbooks and school library books nationwide.

Beverly LaHaye is an influential Christian leader in her own right as head of Concerned Women for America (CWA), a nationwide organization that promotes the conservative Christian political and social agenda. With a strong grassroots organization, the CWA has been able to exert influence on local school boards on curriculum and textbook issues.

James Madison (1751–1836)

Fourth president of the United States and, like Thomas Jefferson, a strong supporter of the separation of church and state, Madison was primarily responsible for drafting the U.S. Constitution and is still cited by the courts when they are considering whether a particular religious practice is appropriate in the public schools. Because it was Madison who drafted the First Amendment, including the religion clauses, his views are especially influential as to their original meaning.

At the time of the American Revolution, Virginia, like many other colonies, used public funds to support its Anglican church. Madison not only opposed such funding but also agitated for complete religious freedom for minorities. Madison set out his arguments in his "Memorial and Remonstrance against Religious Assessments" (1785). Madison's views are implicit in the Constitution. Although all state constitutions mention God, the federal Constitution does not. The sole reference to religion is found in Article IV, forbidding religious tests for public office (membership in a particular religion as a condition of employment).

Madison agreed with Jefferson that there should be a strict wall of separation between religion and the federal government. Although Madison was a strict separationist, he did proclaim national days of thanksgiving.

Vashti McCollum (1913–)

McCollum gained the national spotlight when she filed a lawsuit objecting to the religion classes being given in her son's school in Champaign, Illinois. The students were released early from class, and children with parental permission attended religion classes in their own schools.

The U.S. Supreme Court in *McCollum v. Board of Education* (1948) agreed with McCollum, holding that the teaching of religion on the schoolgrounds violated the establishment clause of the Constitution, which set the stage for all of the later cases that banned religious expression in the public schools. McCollum paid a personal price for her beliefs, later writing that she and her family were harassed during the legal proceedings.

Sandra Day O'Connor (1930–)

The first women to serve on the U.S. Supreme Court, Sandra Day O'Connor graduated from Stanford Law School. Although she graduated at the top of her class, O'Connor was rejected by a number of large law firms. She first worked as a deputy county attorney in California, later in private practice, and then became an Arizona assistant attorney general. Active in politics, O'Connor was appointed and then elected to the Arizona Senate, eventually rising to the position of majority leader. She was next elected a local judge and then appointed to the Arizona Court of Appeals. In 1981, O'Connor was a surprise appointment to the Supreme Court by President Reagan.

On the bench, O'Connor is generally a member of the conservative block, sometimes voting against legislation favoring women and minorities. Justice O'Connor has devised her own test of the separation of church and state. She will normally find a constitutional violation if the school's action amounts to an "endorsement" of the religious practice. She normally adopts a practical case-by-case approach rather than a doctrinaire one.

Madalyn Murray O'Hair (1919–)

Madalyn Murray successfully challenged the reading of the Bible and the recitation of the Lord's Prayer in the Baltimore public schools. Murray was not only an atheist but also a Communist sympathizer who tried unsuccessfully to immigrate with her son William to the Soviet Union in 1959. When this failed, William enrolled in the ninth grade. The routine in the school was to start the day in homeroom with a reading of a verse from the Bible, without comment, recitation of the Lord's Prayer, and the pledge of allegiance to the flag. The school district offered to allow William to avoid attending homeroom, but Murray sued to have the religious activity banned. Murray received moral and financial support in her quest, most notably from the American Civil Liberties Union, which joined the case on Murray's side.

Murray v. Curlett went to the Supreme Court along with a nearly identical Pennsylvania case, *School District of Abington Township v. Schempp* (1963). The Court ruled 8 to 1 that Bible reading and school prayer have no place in public schools as a violation of the establishment clause. Murray—fond of publicity—did nothing to diffuse the resulting controversy. She later went on to run a magazine, *The American Atheist,* and continued to promote atheism. She also was a motivating force behind an organization of the same name. In 1996, she moved to Austin, Texas, and mysteriously disappeared along with $600,000 from the American Atheists. Ironically, William, estranged from his mother, became an evangelical Christian and devoted himself to lobbying for the return of voluntary prayer to the schools.

Thomas Paine (1737–1809)

Paine, a radical political writer, became an overnight celebrity on the publication of his Revolutionary War pamphlet *Common Sense* (1776). The first issue of his series of pamphlets called *The*

Crisis was so inspiring to patriots that Washington ordered it read to his troops at Valley Forge.

Always an advocate of reason and political and individual liberty, Paine is recognized as a leading influence on the Revolution. He believed in the separation of church and state: "As to religion, I hold it to be the indispensable duty of government to protect all conscientious profession thereof, and I know of no other business which government hath to do therewith." Many of his ideas were shared with or borrowed by Jefferson and Madison.

After the revolution, Paine returned first to England where he published *The Rights of Man* (1791/1792), in which he defended the French Revolution and responded to Edmund Burke's *Reflections on the French Revolution.* Charged with treason, Paine fled to France where he became a citizen and a leading figure in the French Revolution. Paine returned to America where he died in poverty.

Charles Pinckney (1757–1824)

One of South Carolina's delegates at the 1787 Constitutional Convention in Philadelphia, Pinckney was a staunch defender of the concept of the separation of church and state. He proposed a motion to forbid the use of religious tests to qualify for federal office, which was incorporated in Article VI of the Constitution.

Pinckney proposed an amendment on the separation of church and state that was not enacted as part of the final document. The amendment provided that "the legislature of the United States shall pass no law on the subject of religion."

Ralph Reed (1961–)

As executive secretary of Pat Robertson's Christian Coalition, Reed become perhaps the most visible conservative Christian leader during the 1980s and early 1990s. Reed was active in conservative politics while still a college student and became even more active after becoming a born-again Christian. In 1989, when evangelist and presidential candidate Pat Robertson formed a new conservative political group, the Christian Coalition, to espouse conservative Christian concerns, he chose young Reed as its executive director. Reed proved to be an able recruiter and spokesperson for the group, whose membership grew to over one million. The return of Christianity and especially prayer to the classroom is a priority item on the coalition's agenda. In some states the coalition was able to elect conservative Christians to school boards with the goal of more religion in the public schools and to select textbooks that would give more attention to conservative Christian values. Local chapters of the organization were able to muster conservative voters to the polls and to exert influence not only on local school boards but on state legislatures as well. In 1997 Ralph Reed resigned as head of the Christian Coalition to pursue other interests.

William H. Rehnquist (1924–)

Chief legal council for the justice department under Richard Nixon, William H. Rehnquist, Jr., was nominated to the Supreme Court by Nixon in 1971, and in 1986 President Reagan nominated him to fill the vacancy of chief justice after Warren Burger's resignation. Although a graduate of Stanford, Harvard, and Stanford Law School, there was significant opposition to his nomination as chief justice because of his political conservatism and close ties to Nixon.

On the Court, Justice Rehnquist has been a consistent conservative, although often in dissent. This has generally been true in the religion in the school cases as well. For example, Rehnquist was in the dissent in the 1992 graduation prayer case (*Lee v. Weisman*).

Pat Robertson (1930–)

Marion Gordon (Pat) Robertson, a Yale Law School graduate and ordained minister, became the best-known television evangelist of his time. Robertson saw the potential for television evangelism earlier than most, and started his Christian Broadcasting Network in 1959. His shows, including fundraising telethons and the popular "700 Club," reached over 100 million viewers in the 1980s. Robertson championed a return to "family values," including a return of prayer to the public schools and tuition tax credits (vouchers) for families who wished to send their children to church-run schools.

Because of his popularity and high name recognition, Robertson attempted to win the Republican nomination for president in 1988. Although he won the Iowa caucus in a surprise upset, he was unable to make any headway in other states and eventually withdrew from the race. In 1989 he established the Christian Coalition, a political group aimed at furthering his own view of family values, including prayer in the schools, tuition tax credits, and texts that discussed creationism alongside the theory of evolution. The Christian Coalition was able to lobby effectively for conservative Christians, especially at the local level. Financial reverses from overseas investments distracted Robertson by 1997.

Antonin Scalia (1936–)

A well-known conservative legal scholar and a graduate of Harvard Law School, Scalia was in private practice before becoming a law professor at the University of Virginia. He was head of the White House Office of Legal Counsel in the Nixon administration and returned to teach at the University of Chicago Law School where he enhanced his reputation as a leading conservative legal scholar. President Reagan appointed Scalia to the very liberal-leaning U.S. Court of Appeals for the District of Columbia and in 1986 to the Supreme Court. On the Court, Scalia has helped forge a solid conservative majority that rejects the judicial activism of the prior fifty years.

Like Chief Justice Rehnquist, Justice Scalia gives broad deference to the views of state legislatures in reviewing laws affecting religious practice in the schools. Although he has frequently been in dissent, he wrote the majority opinion in *Employment Division v. Smith* (1990), which held that religious belief could not excuse commission of a crime (use of peyote by Native Americans).

Phyllis Schlafly (1924–)

Schlafly, a devout Roman Catholic, established a group, the Eagle Forum, in 1975 in response to the Supreme Court's pro-abortion decision in 1973. Schlafly lobbied tirelessly against the Equal Rights Amendment in the late 1970s and gained the approval of many conservative religious leaders.

John Thomas Scopes (1900–1970)

A Tennessee biology teacher who was the defendant in the famous 1925 "monkey trial." Tennessee law forbade the teaching of evolution in any school or university within the state. Scopes, a high school biology teacher in Dayton, Tennessee, decided to bring a test case challenging the law. The ACLU came to his defense, enlisting Clarence Darrow, perhaps the best-known trial attorney of his day. William Jennings Bryan, the noted orator, was attorney for the state of Tennessee. The trial caught the nation's attention and was also followed closely abroad. Bryan, himself a fundamentalist who believed in the literal truth of the depiction in Genesis, railed against Darwin and his theory. Scopes was ultimately convicted and was fined $100, although the conviction was later overturned on a technicality and the fine was never paid. The Tennessee antievolution law was not repealed until 1967. A similar law in Arkansas remained in effect until struck down by the U.S. Supreme Court in 1968.

David Souter (1939–)

A graduate of Harvard University, Harvard Law School, and a Rhodes Scholar at Oxford University, David Souter spent the majority of his legal career in public service. He was assistant deputy attorney general and attorney general in his native New Hampshire. He later became a state judge and was soon appointed to the Supreme Court of New Hampshire. In 1990, Souter was appointed to be a judge on the U.S. Court of Appeals for the First Circuit, but after only two months he was appointed by President Bush to the Supreme Court.

The hardworking Souter quickly established himself as one of the intellectual leaders on the Court and with a moderate bent. His concurring opinion in *Weisman v. Lee* (1992), the case banning invocations at graduation ceremonies, suggests that he will be more of a strict separationist than most of the current justices. In his opinion Souter wrote that in writing the final section of the establishment clause, the founders wanted the government to refrain from promoting all religions, not just a particular religion. Although the majority opinion was based on a showing of coercion, Souter felt that there was no need to show coercion at all: the Constitution simply bars all school-sponsored religious ceremonies.

John Paul Stevens III (1920–)

John Paul Stevens, a native of Chicago, was appointed to the U.S. Court of Appeals for the Seventh Circuit by President Nixon in 1970 after working in private practice for many years. In 1975 he was tapped for the Supreme Court by President Ford. Although he has been termed a moderate, a more apt description might be a maverick with no ideological agenda. Stevens has been a staunch defender of civil rights and a believer in the clear separation of church and state in the public schools.

In recent years Stevens has found himself increasingly in the minority in a number of separation of church and state cases as the majority has retreated from the Court's earlier strict separation. This approach shifts decisionmaking to state legislatures. Stevens has not agreed with this shift and has remained consistent to the principle of strict separation of church and state that the Court developed in the many school cases that it heard during the 1960s and 1970s.

Joseph Storey (1779–1845)

Still regarded as one of the Supreme Court's greatest scholars, Storey is also the youngest person ever appointed to the high court. Appointed to the Court by James Madison, Storey is best-known now for his influential *Commentaries* on American law, including one on the First Amendment that dealt extensively with separation of church and state. Like other individuals in public life at the time, Storey assumed that all citizens would ascribe to the tenets of some religious faith, and, like Madison, he saw no problem with official declarations of days of thanksgiving or invocations asking divine guidance at governmental functions. However, like Madison he was a firm believer that the federal government should show absolutely no preference for one religion over another.

Peter Stuyvesant (1610–1672)

Peter Stuyvesant was the director general of Dutch New York in the middle of the seventeenth century. At the time, Holland was perhaps the most religiously tolerant country in Europe, and Dutch New York was home to a diverse population, including many Jews and Quakers. Stuyvesant, however, imposed strict laws regulating religious practices favoring the Dutch Reformed church. After complaints from colonists, he was quickly overruled by the directors of the Dutch West India Company who reinstated their pluralistic approach to religious practice.

Earl Warren (1891–1974)

Chief Justice of the U.S. Supreme Court, Warren was leader of the influential "Warren Court" (1953–1969) that issued many landmark civil rights and separation of church and state cases. After a career as a crime-fighting attorney general, Warren was elected as a Republican governor of California in 1943, a post he held ten years—from 1942 until his appointment to the Supreme Court. He was an unsuccessful candidate for vice president in 1948, running with Tom Dewey. Although he sought the Republican presidential nomination in 1952, he withdrew and endorsed Eisenhower, the eventual winner. He was nominated for chief justice by Eisenhower, who is reputed to have later termed the nomination "the biggest damn-fool mistake I ever made." Although Warren was a Republican, and at least during his early years in office a conservative governor, he proved a liberal once on the high court.

During his term as chief justice, many of the major cases on religion in the schools were handed down, including *Engel v. Vitale* (1962), which threw out a nondenominational school prayer written by the New York state Board of Regents, and *Abington School District v. Schempp* (1963), which banned Bible reading in public schools. Although the Court's desegregation cases raised the ire of many Americans, the school prayer cases caused an absolute furor. An unsuccessful campaign to impeach Warren was staged and he was vilified as a godless villain by politicians and preachers alike. Although his successor as chief justice—Warren Burger—was a conservative, he continued the Warren Court's separationist agenda.

Warren also headed the commission that investigated the assassination of President Kennedy. He retired from the Court in 1971 and died three years later.

Roger Williams (1603–1683)

Founder of the Rhode Island Colony, Roger Williams was one of the earliest proponents of religious pluralism in North America. A minister in the Massachusetts Bay Colony, Williams was exiled by the leaders of the colony for advocating the separation of church and state: such views were considered "dangerous" by the Puritans of the Bay Colony. Williams headed south and founded what is now Rhode Island, establishing a colony based on separation of church and state and freedom of religion—novel concepts in his day. Williams may have been the first to use the phrase "wall of separation" when referring to the division between the spiritual and secular spheres.

Documents, Court Cases, and Quotations

Documents

Jefferson's Draft Bill for Religious Freedom (1779)

At the time Thomas Jefferson proposed his Bill for Religious Freedom in the Virginia Legislature, it was common for governments to pay the salaries of ministers. The clear distinction between church and state as we know it today simply did not exist. Jefferson's proposal to draw that line was a radical and controversial idea that generated considerable debate. In fact, his bill was not enacted until 1786. With its enactment, Virginia became the first government to commit itself not only to separation of church and state but also to full religious freedom for all its inhabitants. This document inspired the treatment of religion in the U.S. Constitution that still supplies the guiding principles for resolving issues on religion in the schools.

A Bill for Establishing Religious Freedom

SECT. I. Well aware that the opinions and belief of men depend not on their own will, but follow involuntarily the evidence proposed to their minds; that Almighty God hath created the mind free, and manifested his supreme will that free it shall remain by making it altogether insusceptible of restraint; that all attempts to influence it by temporal punishments, or burdens, or by civil incapacitations, tend only to beget habits of hypocrisy and meanness, and are a departure from the plan of the holy author of our religion, who being lord both of body and mind, yet chose not to propagate it by coercions on either, as was in his Almighty power to do, but to extend it by its influence on reason alone; that the impious presumption of legislators and rulers, civil as well as ecclesiastical, who, being themselves but fallible and uninspired men, have assumed dominion over the faith of others, setting up their own opinions and modes of thinking as the only true and infallible, and as such endeavoring to impose them on others, hath established and maintained false religions over the greatest part of the world and through all time: That to compel a man to furnish contributions of money for the propagation of opinions which he disbelieves and abhors, is sinful and tyrannical; that even the forcing him to support this or that teacher of his own religious persuasion, is depriving him of the comfortable liberty of giving his contributions to the particular pastor whose morals he would make his pattern, and whose powers he feels most persuasive to righteousness; and is withdrawing from the ministry those temporary rewards, which proceeding from an approbation of their personal conduct, are an additional incitement to earnest and unremitting labours for the instruction of mankind; that our civil rights have no dependance on our religious opinions, any more than our opinions in physics or geometry; that therefore the proscribing any citizen as unworthy the public confidence by laying upon him an incapacity of being called to offices of trust and emolument, unless he profess or renounce this or that religious opinion, is depriving him injuriously of those privileges and advantages to which, in common with his fellow citizens, he has a natural right; that it tends also to corrupt the principles of that very religion it is meant to encourage, by bribing, with a monopoly of worldly honours and emoluments, those who will externally profess and conform to it; that though indeed these are criminal who do not withstand such temptation, yet neither are those innocent who lay the bait in their way; that the opinions of men are not the object of civil government, nor under its jurisdiction; that to suffer the civil magistrate to intrude his powers into the field of opinion and to restrain the profession or propagation of principles on supposition of their ill tendency is a dangerous falacy, which at once destroys all religious liberty, because he being of course judge of that tendency will make his opinions the rule of judgment, and approve or condemn the sentiments of others only as they shall square with or differ from his own; that it is time enough for the rightful purposes of civil government for its officers to interfere when principles break out into overt acts against peace and good order; and finally, that truth is great and will prevail if left to herself; that she is the proper and sufficient antagonist to error, and has nothing to fear from the conflict unless by human interposition disarmed of her natural weapons, free argument and debate; errors ceasing to be dangerous when it is permitted freely to contradict them.

SECT. II. WE the General Assembly of Virginia do enact that no man shall be compelled to frequent or support any religious worship, place, or ministry whatsoever, nor shall be enforced, restrained, molested, or burthened in his body or goods, nor shall otherwise suffer, on account of his religious opinions or belief; but that all men shall be free to profess, and by argument to maintain, their opinions in matters of religion, and that the same shall in no wise diminish, enlarge, or affect their civil capacities.

SECT. III. AND though we well know that this Assembly, elected by the people for the ordinary purposes of legislation only, have no power to restrain the acts of succeeding Assemblies, constituted with powers equal to our own, and that therefore to declare this act irrevocable would be of no effect in law; yet we are free to declare, and do declare, that the rights hereby asserted are of the natural rights of mankind, and that if any act shall be hereafter passed to repeal the present or to narrow its operation, such act will be an infringement of natural right.

Madison's Memorial and Remonstrance

James Madison, primary author of the U.S. Constitution and later U.S. President, penned this reply to Patrick Henry's proposal in the Virginia Legislature that public monies be used to pay the salaries of teachers of the Christian religion. This is one of the earliest U.S. documents speaking directly to the issue of separation of church and state in the schools. In Madison's view, allowing government support of this teaching would infringe on the rights of religious minorities in Virginia. Madison's view prevailed and Patrick Henry's proposal was defeated. Shortly thereafter the legislature approved Thomas Jefferson's Bill for Religious Freedom.

To the Honorable the General Assembly of the Commonwealth of Virginia

Memorial and Remonstrance

We the subscribers, citizens of the said Commonwealth, having taken into serious consideration, a Bill printed by order of the last Session of General Assembly, entitled "A Bill establishing a provision for Teachers of the Christian Religion," and conceiving that the same if finally armed with the sanctions of a law, will be a dangerous abuse of power, are bound as faithful members of a free State to remonstrate against it, and to declare the reasons by which we are determined. We remonstrate against the said Bill,

1. Because we hold it for a fundamental and undeniable truth, "that religion or the duty which we owe to our Creator and the manner of discharging it, can be directed only by reason and conviction, not by force or violence." The Religion then of every man must be left to the conviction and conscience of every man; and it is the right of every man to exercise it as these may dictate.

This right is in its nature an unalienable right. It is unalienable, because the opinions of men, depending only on the evidence contemplated by their own minds cannot follow the dictates of other men: It is unalienable also, because what is here a right towards men, is a duty towards the Creator.

It is the duty of every man to render to the Creator such homage and such only as he believes to be acceptable to him. This duty is precedent, both in order of time and in degree of obligation, to the claims of Civil Society. Before any man can be considered as a member of Civil Society, he must be considered as a subject of the Governor of the Universe: And if a member of Civil Society, do it with a saving of his allegiance to the Universal Sovereign.

We maintain therefore that in matters of Religion, no man's right is abridged by the institution of Civil Society and that Religion is wholly exempt from its cognizance. True it is, that no other rule exists, by which any question which may divide a

Society, can be ultimately determined, but the will of the majority; but it is also true that the majority may trespass on the rights of the minority.

2. Because Religion be exempt from the authority of the Society at large, still less can it be subject to that of the Legislative Body. The latter are but the creatures and vicegerents of the former. Their jurisdiction is both derivative and limited: it is limited with regard to the co-ordinate departments, more necessarily is it limited with regard to the constituents.

The preservation of a free Government requires not merely, that the metes and bounds which separate each department of power be invariably maintained; but more especially that neither of them be suffered to overleap the great Barrier which defends the rights of the people. The Rulers who are guilty of such an encroachment, exceed the commission from which they derive their authority, and are Tyrants. The People who submit to it are governed by laws made neither by themselves nor by an authority derived from them, and are slaves.

3. Because it is proper to take alarm at the first experiment on our liberties. We hold this prudent jealousy to be the first duty of Citizens, and one of the noblest characteristics of the late Revolution. The free men of America did not wait till usurped power had strengthened itself by exercise, and entangled the question in precedents. They saw all the consequences in the principle, and they avoided the consequences by denying the principle. We revere this lesson too much soon to forget it.

Who does not see that the same authority which can establish Christianity, in exclusion of all other Religions, may establish with the same ease any particular sect of Christians, in exclusion of all other Sects? That the same authority which can force a citizen to contribute three pence only of his property for the support of any one establishment, may force him to conform to any other establishment in all cases whatsoever?

4. Because the Bill violates the equality which ought to be the basis of every law, and which is more indispensable, in proportion as the validity or expediency of any law is more liable to be impeached. If "all men are by nature equally free and independent," all men are to be considered as entering into Society on equal conditions; as relinquishing no more, and therefore retaining no less, one than another, of their natural rights.

Above all they are to be considered as retaining an "equal title to the free exercise of Religion according to the dictates of Conscience." Whilst we assert for ourselves a freedom to embrace, to profess and to observe the Religion which we believe to be of divine origin, we cannot deny an equal freedom to those whose minds have not yet yielded to the evidence which has convinced us.

If this freedom be abused, it is an offence against God, not against man: To God, therefore, not to man, must an account of it be rendered. As the Bill violates equality by subjecting some to peculiar burdens, so it violates the same principle, by granting to others peculiar exemptions. Are the quakers and Menonists the only sects who think a compulsive support of their Religions unnecessary and unwarrantable? Can their piety alone be entrusted with the care of public worship? Ought their Religions to be endowed above all others with extraordinary privileges by which proselytes may be enticed from all others?

We think too favorably of the justice and good sense of these denominations to believe that they either covet pre-eminences over their fellow citizens or that they will be seduced by them from the common opposition to the measure.

5. Because the Bill implies either that the Civil Magistrate is a competent Judge of Religious Truth; or that he may employ Religion as an engine of Civil policy. The first is an arrogant pretension falsified by the contradictory opinions of Rulers in all ages, and throughout the world: the second an unhallowed perversion of the means of salvation.

6. Because the establishment proposed by the Bill is not requisite for the support of the Christian Religion. To say that it is, is a contradiction to the Christian Religion itself, for every page of it disavows a dependence on the powers of this world: it is a contradiction to fact; for it is known that this Religion both existed and flourished, not only without the support of human laws, but in spite of every opposition from them, and not only during the period of miraculous aid, but long after it had been left to its own evidence and the ordinary care of Providence.

Nay, it is a contradiction in terms; for a Religion not invented by human policy, must have pre-existed and been supported, before it was established by human policy. It is moreover to weaken in those who profess this Religion a pious confidence in its innate excellence and the patronage of its Author; and to foster in those who still reject it, a suspicion that its friends are too conscious of its fallacies to trust it to its own merits.

7. Because experience witnesseth that ecclesiastical establishments, instead of maintaining the purity and efficacy of Religion, have had a contrary operation.

During almost fifteen centuries has the legal establishment of Christianity been on trial. What have been its fruits? More or less in all places, pride and indolence in the Clergy, ignorance and servility in the laity, in both, superstition, bigotry and persecution. Enquire of the Teachers of Christianity for the ages in which it appeared in its greatest luster; those of every sect, point to the ages prior to its incorporation with Civil policy.

Propose a restoration of this primitive State in which its Teachers depended on the voluntary rewards of their flocks, many of them predict its downfall. On which Side ought their testimony to have greatest weight, when for or when against their interest?

8. Because the establishment in question is not necessary for the support of Civil Government. If it be urged as necessary for the support of Civil Government only as it is a means of supporting Religion, and it be not necessary for the latter purpose, it cannot be necessary for the former. If Religion be not within the cognizance of Civil Government how can its legal establishment be necessary to Civil Government? What influence in fact have ecclesiastical establishments had on Civil Society?

In some instances they have been seen to erect a spiritual tyranny on the ruins of the Civil authority; in many instances they have been seen upholding the thrones of political tyranny: in no instance have they been seen the guardians of the liberties of the people. Rulers who wished to subvert the public liberty, may have found an established Clergy convenient auxiliaries.

A just Government instituted to secure & perpetuate it needs them not. Such a Government will be best supported by protecting every Citizen in the enjoyment of his Religion with the same equal hand which protects his person and his property; by neither invading the equal rights of any Sect, nor suffering any Sect to invade those of another.

9. Because the proposed establishment is a departure from the generous policy, which, offering an Asylum to the persecuted and oppressed of every Nation and Religion, promised a luster to our country, and an accession to the number of its citizens. What a melancholy mark is the Bill of sudden degeneracy? Instead of holding forth an Asylum to the persecuted, it is itself a signal of persecution.

It degrades from the equal rank of Citizens all those who see opinions in Religion do not bend to those of the Legislative authority. Distant as it may be in its present form from the Inquisition, it differs from it only in degree. The one is the first step, the other the last in the career of intolerance. The magnanimous sufferer under this cruel scourge in foreign Regions, must view the Bill as a Beacon on our Coast, warning him to seek some other haven, where liberty and philanthropy in their due extent, may offer a more certain repose from his Troubles.

10. Because it will have a like tendency to banish our Citizens. The allurements presented by other situations are every day thinning their number. To superadd a fresh motive to emigration by revoking the liberty which they now enjoy, would be the same species of folly which has dishonored and depopulated flourishing kingdoms.

11. Because it will destroy that moderation and harmony which the forbearance of our laws to intermeddle with Religion has produced among its several sects. Torrents of blood have been spilt in the old world, by vain attempts of the secular arm, to extinguish Religious discord, by proscribing all difference in Religious opinion. Time has at length revealed the true remedy. Every relaxation of narrow and rigorous policy, wherever it has been tried, has been found to assuage the disease.

The American Theater has exhibited proofs that equal and complete liberty, if it does not wholly eradicate it, sufficiently destroys its malignant influence on the health and prosperity of the State. If with the salutary effects of this system under our own eyes, we begin to contract the bounds of Religious freedom, we know no name that will too severely reproach our folly. At least let warning be taken at the first fruits of the threatened innovation.

The very appearance of the Bill has transformed "that Christian forbearance, love and charity," which of late mutually prevailed, into animosities and jealousies, which may not soon be appeased. What mischiefs may not be dreaded, should this enemy to the public quiet be armed with the force of a law?

12. Because the policy of the Bill is adverse to the diffusion of the light of Christianity. The first wish of those who enjoy this precious gift ought to be that it may be imparted to the whole race of mankind. Compare the number of those who have as yet received it with the number still remaining under the dominion of false Religions; and how small is the former! Does the policy of the Bill tend to lessen the disproportion?

No; it at once discourages those who are strangers to the light of revelation from coming into the Region of it; and countenances by example the nations who continue in darkness, in shutting out those who might convey it to them. Instead of

Leveling as far as possible, every obstacle to the victorious progress of Truth, the Bill with an ignoble and unchristian timidity would circumscribe it with a wall of defense against the encroachments of error.

13. Because attempts to enforce by legal sanctions, acts obnoxious to so great a proportion of Citizens, tend to enervate the laws in general, and to slacken the bands of Society. If it be difficult to execute any law which is not generally deemed necessary or salutary, what must be the case, where it is deemed invalid and dangerous? And what may be the effect of so striking an example of impotency in the Government, on its general authority?

14. Because a measure of such singular magnitude and delicacy ought not to be imposed, without the clearest evidence that it is called for by a majority of citizens, and no satisfactory method is yet proposed by which the voice of the majority in this case may be determined, or its influence secured.

The people of the respective counties are indeed requested to signify their opinion respecting the adoption of the Bill to the next Session of Assembly. But the representatives of the Counties will be that of the people. Our hope is that neither of the former will, after due consideration, espouse the dangerous principle of the Bill. Should the event disappoint us, it will still leave us in full confidence, that a fair appeal to the latter will reverse the sentence against our liberties.

15. Because finally, "the equal right of every citizen to the free exercise of his Religion according to the dictates of conscience" is held by the same tenure with all our other rights.

If we recur to its origin, it is equally the gift of nature; if we weigh its importance, it cannot be less dear to us; if we consult the "Declaration of those rights which pertain to the good people of Virginia, as the basis and foundation of Government," it is enumerated with equal solemnity, or rather studied emphasis.

Either then, we must say, that the Will of the Legislature is the only measure of their authority; and that in the plenitude of this authority, they may sweep away all our fundamental rights; or, that they are bound to leave this particular right untouched and sacred:

Either we must say, that they may control the freedom of the press, may abolish the Trial by Jury, may swallow up the Executive and Judiciary Powers of the State; nay that they may despoil us of our very right of suffrage, and erect themselves into an independent and hereditary Assembly or, we must say, that they have no authority to enact into the law the Bill under consideration.

Conclusion:

We the Subscribers say, that the General Assembly of this Commonwealth have no such authority: And that no effort may be omitted on our part against so dangerous an usurpation, we oppose to it, this remonstrance; earnestly praying, as we are in duty bound, that the Supreme Lawgiver of the Universe, by illuminating those to whom it is addressed, may on the one hand, turn their Councils from every act which would affront his holy prerogative, or violate the trust committed to them: and on the other, guide them into every measure which may be worthy of his [blessing, may re]bound to their own praise, and may establish more firmly the liberties, the prosperity and the happiness of the Commonwealth.

Federal Equal Access Act

The federal Equal Access Act (1984) prohibits discrimination against student groups on the basis of religious, political, or philosophical views. If a public school allows other "noncurriculum-related groups" to use school facilities, then the school must also allow religious clubs equal access.

4071. Denial of equal access prohibited

(a) Restriction of limited open forum on basis of religious, political, philosophical, or other speech content prohibited

It shall be unlawful for any public secondary school which receives Federal financial assistance and which has a limited open forum to deny equal access or a fair opportunity to, or discriminate against, any students who wish to conduct a meeting within that limited open forum on the basis of the religious, political, philosophical, or other content of the speech at such meetings.

(b) "Limited open forum" defined

A public secondary school has a limited open forum whenever such school grants an offering to or opportunity for one or more noncurriculum-related student groups to meet on school premises during noninstructional time.

(c) Fair opportunity criteria

Schools shall be deemed to offer a fair opportunity to students who wish to conduct a meeting within its limited open forum if such a school uniformly provides that—

(1) the meeting is voluntary and student-initiated;

(2) there is no sponsorship of the meeting by the school, the government, or its agents or employees;

(3) employees or agents of the school or government are present at religious meetings only in a nonparticipatory capacity;

(4) the meeting does not materially and substantially interfere with the orderly conduct of educational activities within the school; and

(5) nonschool persons may not direct, conduct, control, or regularly attend activities of student groups.

(d) Construction of subchapter with respect to certain rights

Nothing in this subchapter shall be construed to authorize the United States or any State or political subdivision thereof—

(1) to influence the form or content of any prayer or other religious activity;

(2) to require any person to participate in prayer or other religious activity;

(3) to expend public funds beyond the incidental cost of providing the space for student-initiated meetings;

(4) to compel any school agent or employee to attend a school meeting if the content of the speech at the meeting is contrary to the beliefs of the agent or employee;

(5) to sanction meetings that are otherwise unlawful;

(6) to limit the rights of groups of students which are not of a specified numerical size; or

(7) to abridge the constitutional rights of any person.

(e) Federal financial assistance to schools unaffected

Notwithstanding the availability of any other remedy under the Constitution or the laws of the United States, nothing in this subchapter shall be construed to authorize the United States to deny or withhold Federal financial assistance to any school.

(f) Authority of schools with respect to order, discipline, well-being, and attendance concerns

Nothing in this subchapter shall be construed to limit the authority of the school, its agents or employees, to maintain order and discipline on school premises, to protect the well-being of students and faculty, and to assure that attendance of students at meetings is voluntary.

Federal Religious Freedom Restoration Act of 1993

This federal law was passed by an overwhelming majority of votes in 1993 after the Supreme Court's decision in *Employment Division v. Smith*. Church leaders were alarmed that the holding in the *Smith* case would allow the government to pass laws restricting religious practice and the law was intended to protect religious activity. The act itself was declared unconstitutional in *Boerne v. Flores* in 1997. However, it is likely that the Congress will redraft and pass a revised version of this act.

H.R.1308

One Hundred Third Congress of the United States of America at the First Session Begun and held at the City of Washington on Tuesday, the fifth day of January, one thousand nine hundred and ninety-three An Act

TITLE: To protect the free exercise of religion.

Be it enacted by the Senate and House of Representatives of the United States of America in Congress assembled,

SEC. 1. SHORT TITLE.

This Act may be cited as the 'Religious Freedom Restoration Act of 1993.'

SEC. 2. CONGRESSIONAL FINDINGS AND DECLARATION OF PURPOSES.

(a) Findings: The Congress finds that—

(1) the framers of the Constitution, recognizing free exercise of religion as an unalienable right, secured its protection in the First Amendment to the Constitution;

(2) laws 'neutral' toward religion may burden religious exercise as surely as laws intended to interfere with religious exercise;

(3) governments should not substantially burden religious exercise without compelling justification;

(4) in *Employment Division v. Smith*, 494 U.S. 872 (1990) the Supreme Court virtually eliminated the requirement that the government justify burdens on religious exercise imposed by laws neutral toward religion; and

(5) the compelling interest test as set forth in prior Federal court rulings is a workable test for striking sensible balances be-

tween religious liberty and competing prior governmental interests.

(b) Purposes: The purposes of this Act are—

(1) to restore the compelling interest test as set forth in *Sherbert v. Verner*, 374 U.S. 398 (1963) and *Wisconsin v. Yoder*, 406 U.S. 205 (1972) and to guarantee its application in all cases where free exercise of religion is substantially burdened; and

(2) to provide a claim or defense to persons whose religious exercise is substantially burdened by government.

SEC. 3. FREE EXERCISE OF RELIGION PROTECTED.

(a) In General: Government shall not substantially burden a person's exercise of religion even if the burden results from a rule of general applicability, except as provided in subsection (b).

(b) Exception: Government may substantially burden a person's exercise of religion only if it demonstrates that application of the burden to the person—

(1) is in furtherance of a compelling governmental interest; and

(2) is the least restrictive means of furthering that compelling governmental interest.

(c) Judicial Relief: A person whose religious exercise has been burdened in violation of this section may assert that violation as a claim or defense in a judicial proceeding and obtain appropriate relief against a government. Standing to assert a claim or defense under this section shall be governed by the general rules of standing under article III of the Constitution.

SEC. 4. ATTORNEYS FEES.

(a) Judicial Proceedings: Section 722 of the Revised Statutes (42 U.S.C. 1988) is amended by inserting 'the Religious Freedom Restoration Act of 1993,' before 'or title VI of the Civil Rights Act of 1964.'

(b) Administrative Proceedings: Section 504(b)(1)(C) of title 5, United States Code, is amended—

(1) by striking 'and' at the end of clause (ii);

(2) by striking the semicolon at the end of clause (iii) and inserting ', and'; and

(3) by inserting '(iv) the Religious Freedom Restoration Act of 1993;' after clause (iii).

SEC. 5. DEFINITIONS.

As used in this Act—

(1) the term 'government' includes a branch, department, agency, instrumentality, and official (or other person acting

under color of law) of the United States, a State, or a subdivision of a State;

(2) the term 'State' includes the District of Columbia, the Commonwealth of Puerto Rico, and each territory and possession of the United States;

(3) the term 'demonstrates' means meets the burdens of going forward with the evidence and of persuasion; and

(4) the term 'exercise of religion' means the exercise of religion under the First Amendment to the Constitution.

SEC. 6. APPLICABILITY.

(a) In General. This Act applies to all Federal and State law, and the implementation of that law, whether statutory or otherwise, and whether adopted before or after the enactment of this Act.

(b) Rule of Construction. Federal statutory law adopted after the date of the enactment of this Act is subject to this Act unless such law explicitly excludes such application by reference to this Act.

(c) Religious Belief Unaffected. Nothing in this Act shall be construed to authorize any government to burden any religious belief.

SEC. 7. ESTABLISHMENT CLAUSE UNAFFECTED.

Nothing in this Act shall be construed to affect, interpret, or in any way address that portion of the First Amendment prohibiting laws respecting the establishment of religion (referred to in this section as the 'Establishment Clause'). Granting government funding, benefits, or exemptions, to the extent permissible under the Establishment Clause, shall not constitute a violation of this Act. As used in this section, the term 'granting,' used with respect to government funding, benefits, or exemptions, does not include the denial of government funding, benefits, or exemptions.

President Clinton's Speech on Religious Liberty in America

The following is the text of a July 1995 speech by President William Clinton in which he discussed many of the issues concerning religion in the schools. The speech details the development and importance of the separation of church and state, discusses some of the important court decisions, and suggests practical solutions for dealing with religious expression in the schools. The speech also outlines the guidelines suggested by the federal Department of Education for schools dealing with these issues.

Remarks by the President on Religious Liberty in America James Madison High School Vienna, Virginia 10:58 a.m. EDT

The President: Thank you, Secretary Riley, for the introduction, but more for your outstanding leadership of the Department of Education and the work you have done not only to increase the investment of our country in education, but also to lift the quality and the standards of education and to deal forthrightly with some of the more difficult, but important issues in education that go to the heart of the character of the young people we build in our country.

Superintendent Spillane, congratulations on your award and the work you are doing here in this district. Dr. Clark, Ms. Lubetkin. To Danny Murphy, I thought he gave such a good speech I could imagine him on a lot of platforms in the years ahead. (Laughter.) He did a very fine job.

Mayor Robinson, and to the Board of Supervisors, Chair Katherine Hanley, and to all the religious leaders, parents, students who are here; the teachers; and especially to the James Madison teachers, thank you for coming today.

Last week at my alma mater, Georgetown, I had a chance to do something that I hope to do more often as President, to have a genuine conversation with the American people about the best way for us to move forward as a nation and to resolve some of the great questions that are nagging at us today. I believe, as I have said repeatedly, that our nation faces two great challenges: first of all, to restore the American dream of opportunity, and the American tradition of responsibility; and second, to bring our country together amidst all of our diversity in a stronger community so that we can find common ground and move forward together.

In my first two years as President I worked harder on the first question, how to get the economy going, how to deal with the specific problems of the country, how to inspire more responsibility through things like welfare reform and child support enforcement. But I have come to believe that unless we can solve the second problem we'll never really solve the first one. Unless we can find a way to honestly and openly debate our differences and find common ground, to celebrate all the diversity of America and still give people a chance to live in the way they think is right, so that we are stronger for our differences, not weaker, we won't be able to meet the economic and other challenges before us. And therefore, I have decided that I should spend some more time in some conversations about things Americans care a lot about and that they're deeply divided over.

Today I want to talk about a conversation—about a subject that can provoke a fight in nearly any country town or on any city street corner in America—religion. It's a subject that should not drive us apart. And we have a mechanism as old as our Constitution for bringing us together.

This country, after all, was founded by people of profound faith who mentioned Divine Providence and the guidance of God twice in the Declaration of Independence. They were searching for a place to express their faith freely without persecution. We take it for granted today that that's so in this country, but it was not always so. And it certainly has not always been so across the world. Many of the people who were our first settlers came here primarily because they were looking for a place where they could practice their faith without being persecuted by the government.

Here in Virginia's soil, as the Secretary of Education has said, the oldest and deepest roots of religious liberty can be found. The First Amendment was modeled on Thomas Jefferson's Statutes of Religious Liberty for Virginia. He thought so much of it that he asked that on his gravestone it be said not that he was President, not that he had been Vice President or Secretary of State, but that he was the founder of the University of Virginia, the author of the Declaration of Independence and the author of the Statutes of Religious Liberty for the state of Virginia.

And of course, no one did more than James Madison to put the entire Bill of Rights in our Constitution, and especially, the First Amendment.

Religious freedom is literally our first freedom. It is the first thing mentioned in the Declaration of Independence. And as it opens, it says Congress cannot make a law that either establishes a religion or restricts the free exercise of religion. Now, as with every provision of our Constitution, that law has had to be interpreted over the years, and it has in various ways that some of us agree with and some of us disagree with. But one thing is indisputable: the First Amendment has protected our freedom to be religious or not religious, as we choose, with the consequence that in this highly secular age the United States is clearly the most conventionally religious country in the entire world, at least the entire industrialized world.

We have more than 250,000 places of worship. More people go to church here every week, or to synagogue, or to a mosque or other place of worship than in any other country in the world. More people believe religion is directly important to their lives than in any other advanced, industrialized country in the world. And it is not an accident. It is something that has always been a part of our life.

I grew up in Arkansas which is, except for West Virginia, probably the state that's most heavily Southern Baptist Protestant in the country. But we had two synagogues and a Greek Orthodox church in my hometown. Not so long ago in the heart of our agricultural country in Eastern Arkansas one of our universities did a big outreach to students in the Middle East, and before you know it, out there on this flat land where there was no building more than two stories high, there rose a great mosque. And all the farmers from miles around drove in to see what the mosque was like and try to figure out what was going on there. (Laughter.)

This is a remarkable country. And I have tried to be faithful to that tradition that we have of the First Amendment. It's something that's very important to me.

Secretary Riley mentioned when I was at Georgetown, Georgetown is a Jesuit school, a Catholic school. All the Catholics were required to teach theology, and those of us who weren't Catholic took a course in world's religion, which we called Buddhism for Baptists. (Laughter.) And I began a sort of love affair with the religions that I did not know anything about before that time.

It's a personal thing to me because of my own religious faith and the faith of my family. And I've always felt that in order for me to be free to practice my faith in this country, I had to let other people be as free as possible to practice theirs, and that the government had an extraordinary obligation to bend over backwards not to do anything to impose any set of views on any group of people or to allow others to do it under the cover of law.

That's why I was very proud—one of the proudest things I've been able to do as President was to sign into law the Religious Freedom Restoration Act in 1993. And it was designed to reverse the decision of the Supreme Court that essentially made it pretty easy for government, in the pursuit of its legitimate objectives, to restrict the exercise of people's religious liberties. This law basically said—I won't use the legalese—the bottom line was that if the government is going to restrict anybody's legitimate exercise of religion they have to have an extraordinarily good reason and no other way to achieve their compelling objective other than to do this. You have to bend over backwards to avoid getting in the way of people's legitimate exercise of their religious convictions. That's what that law said.

This is something I've tried to do throughout my career. When I was governor, for example, we were having—of Arkansas in the '80s—you may remember this—there were religious leaders going to jail in America because they ran child care centers that they refused to have certified by the state because they said it undermined their ministry. We solved that problem in our state. There were people who were prepared to go to jail over the home schooling issue in the '80s because they said it was part of their religious ministry. We solved that problem in our state.

With the Religious Freedom Restoration Act we made it possible, clearly, in areas that were previously ambiguous for Native Americans, for American Jews, for Muslims to practice the full range of their religious practices when they might have otherwise come in contact with some governmental regulation.

And in a case that was quite important to the Evangelicals in our country, I instructed the Justice Department to change our position after the law passed on a tithing case where a family had been tithing to their church and the man declared bankruptcy, and the government took the position they could go get the money away from the church because he knew he was bankrupt at the time he gave it. And I realized in some ways that was a close question, but I thought we had to stand up for the proposition that people should be able to practice their religious convictions.

Secretary Riley and I, in another context, have also learned as we have gone along in this work that all the religions obviously share a certain devotion to a certain set of values which make a big difference in the schools. I want to commend Secretary Riley for his relentless support of the so-called character education movement in our schools, which is clearly led in many schools that had great troubles to reduce drop-out rates, increased performance in schools, better citizenship in ways that didn't promote any particular religious views but at least unapologetically advocated values shared by all major religions.

In this school, one of the reasons I wanted to come here is because I recognize that this work has been done here. There's a course in this school called Combating Intolerance, which deals not only with racial issues, but also with religious differences, and studies times in the past when people have been killed in mass numbers and persecuted because of their religious convictions.

You can make a compelling argument that the tragic war in Bosnia today is more of a religious war than an ethnic war. The truth is, biologically, there is no difference in the Serbs, the Croats, and the Muslims. They are Catholics, Orthodox Christians, and Muslims, and they are so for historic reasons. But it's really more of a religious war than an ethnic war when properly viewed. And I think it's very important that the people in this school are learning that and, in the process, will come back to that every great religion teaches honesty and trustworthiness and responsibility and devotion to family, and charity and compassion toward others.

Our sense of our own religion and our respect for others has really helped us to work together for two centuries. It's made a big difference in the way we live and the way we function and our ability to overcome adversity. The Constitution wouldn't be what it is without James Madison's religious values. But it's also, frankly, given us a lot of elbow room. I remember, for example, that Abraham Lincoln was derided by his opponents because he belonged to no organized church. But if you read his writings and you study what happened to him, especially after he came to the White House, he might have had more spiritual depth than any person ever to hold the office that I now have the privilege to occupy.

So we have followed this balance, and it has served us well. Now what I want to talk to you about for a minute is that our Founders understood that religious freedom basically was a coin with two sides. The Constitution protected the free exercise of religion, but prohibited the establishment of religion. It's a careful balance that's uniquely American. It is the genius of the First Amendment. It does not, as some people have implied, make us a religion-free country. It has made us the most religious country in the world.

It does not convert—let's just take the areas of greatest controversy now—all the fights have come over 200 years over what those two things mean: What does it mean for the government to establish a religion, and what does it mean for a government to interfere with the free exercise of religion. The Religious Freedom Restoration Act was designed to clarify the second provision—government interfering with the free exercise of religion and to say you can do that almost never. You can do that almost never. (Applause.)

We have had a lot more fights in the last 30 years over what the government establishment of religion means. And that's what the whole debate is now over the issue of school prayer, religious practices in the schools and things of that kind. And I want to talk about it because our schools are the places where so much of our hearts are in America and all of our futures are. And I'd like to begin by just sort of pointing out what's going on today and then discussing it if I could. And, again, this is always kind of inflammatory; I want to have a noninflammatory talk about it. (Laughter.)

First of all, let me tell you a little about my personal history. Before the Supreme Court's decision in Engel against Vitale, which said that the state of New York could not write a prayer that had to be said in every school in New York every day, school prayer was as common as apple pie in my hometown. And when I was in junior high school, it was my responsibility either to start every day by reading the Bible or get somebody else to do it. Needless to say, I exerted a lot of energy in finding someone else to do it from time to time, being a normal 13-year-old boy.

Now, you could say, well, it certainly didn't do any harm; it might have done a little good. But remember what I told you. We had two synagogues in my hometown. We also had pretended to be deeply religious and there were no blacks in my school, they were in a segregated school. And I can tell you that all of us who were in there doing it never gave a second thought most of the time to the fact that we didn't have blacks in our schools and that there were Jews in the classroom who were probably deeply offended by half the stuff we were saying or doing—or maybe made to feel inferior.

I say that to make the point that we have not become less religious over the last 30 years by saying that schools cannot impose a particular religion, even if it's a Christian religion and 98 percent of the kids in the schools are Christian and Protestant.

I'm not sure the Catholics were always comfortable with what we did either. We had a big Catholic population in my school and in my hometown. But I did that—I have been a part of this debate we are talking about. This is a part of my personal life experience. So I have seen a lot of progress made and I agreed with the Supreme Court's original decision in *Engel v. Vitale.*

Now, since then, I've not always agreed with every decision the Supreme Court made in the area of the First Amendment. I said the other day I didn't think the decision on the prayer at the commencement, where the Rabbi was asked to give the nonsectarian prayer at the commencement—I didn't agree with that because I didn't think it any coercion at all. And I thought that people were not interfered with. And I didn't think it amounted to the establishment of a religious practice by the government. So I have not always agreed.

But I do believe that on balance, the direction of the First Amendment has been very good for America and has made us the most religious country in the world by keeping the government out of creating religion, supporting particular religions, interfering, and interfering with other people's religious practices.

What is giving rise to so much of this debate today I think is two things. One is the feeling that the schools are special and a lot of kids are in trouble, and a lot of kids are in trouble for nonacademic reasons, and we want our kids to have good values and have a good future.

Let me give you just one example. There is today, being released, a new study of drug use among young people by the group that Joe Califano was associated with—Council for a Drug-Free America—a massive poll of young people themselves. It's a fascinating study and I urge all of you to get it. Joe came in a couple of days ago and briefed me on it. It shows disturbingly that even though serious drug use is down overall in groups in America, casual drug use is coming back up among some of our young people who no longer believe that it's dangerous and have forgotten that's it's wrong and are basically living in a world that I think is very destructive.

And I see it all the time. It's coming back up. Even though we're investing money and trying to combat it in education and treatment programs, and supporting things like the DARE program. And we're breaking more drug rings than ever before around the world. It's almost—it's very disturbing because it's fundamentally something that is kind of creeping back in.

But the study shows that there are three major causes for

young people not using drugs. One is they believe that their future depends upon their not doing it; they're optimistic about the future. The more optimistic kids are about the future, the less likely they are to use drugs.

Second is having a strong, positive relationship with their parents. The closer kids are to their parents and the more tuned in to them they are, and the more their parents are good role models, the less likely kids are to use drugs.

You know what the third is? How religious the children are. The more religious the children are, the less likely they are to use drugs.

So what's the big fight over religion in the schools and what does it mean to us and why are people so upset about it? I think there are basically three reasons. One is, people believe that—most Americans believe that—if you're religious, personally religious, you ought to be able to manifest that anywhere at any time, in a public or private place. Second, I think that most Americans are disturbed if they think that our government is becoming anti-religious, instead of adhering to the firm spirit of the First Amendment—don't establish, don't interfere with, but respect. And the third thing is people worry about our national character as manifest in the lives of our children. The crime rate is going down in almost every major area in America today, but the rate of violent random crime among very young people is still going up.

So these questions take on a certain urgency today for personal reasons and for larger social reasons. And this old debate that Madison and Jefferson started over 200 years ago is still being spun out today basically as it relates to what can and cannot be done in our schools, and the whole question, specific question, of school prayer, although I would argue it goes way beyond that.

So let me tell you what I think the law is and what we're trying to do about it, since I like the First Amendment, and I think we're better off because of it, and I think that if you have two great pillars—the government can't establish and the government can't interfere with—obviously there are going to be a thousand different factual cases that will arise at any given time, and the courts from time to time will make decisions that we don't all agree with, but the question is, are the pillars the right pillars, and do we more or less come out in the right place over the long run.

The Supreme Court is like everybody else, it's imperfect—and so are we. Maybe they're right and we're wrong. But we are going to have these differences. The fundamental balance that has been struck it seems to me has been very good for America, but what is not good today is that people assume that there is a positive-antireligious bias in the cumulative impact of these court decisions with which our administration—the Justice Department and the Secretary of Education and the President—strongly disagree. So let me tell you what I think the law is today and what I have instructed the Department of Education and the Department of Justice to do about it.

The First Amendment does not—I will say again—does not convert our schools into religion-free zones. If a student is told he can't wear a yarmulke, for example, we have an obligation to tell the school the law says the student can, most definitely, wear a yarmulke to school. If a student is told she cannot bring a Bible to school, we have to tell the school, no, the law guarantees her the right to bring the Bible to school.

There are those who do believe our schools should be value neutral and that religion has no place inside the schools. But I think that wrongly interprets the idea of the wall between church and state. They are not the walls of the school.

There are those who say that values and morals and religions have no place in public education; I think that is wrong. First of all, the consequences of having no values are not neutral. The violence in our streets—not value neutral. The movies we see aren't value neutral. Television is not value neutral. Too often we see expressions of human degradation, immorality, violence, and debasement of the human soul that have more influence and take more time and occupy more space in the minds of our young people than any of the influences that are felt at school anyway. Our schools, therefore, must be a barricade against this kind of degradation. And we can do it without violating the First Amendment.

I am deeply troubled that so many Americans feel that their faith is threatened by the mechanisms that are designed to protect their faith. Over the past decade we have seen a real rise in these kind of cultural tensions in America. Some people even say we have a culture war. There have been books written about culture war, the culture of disbelief, all these sort of trends arguing that many Americans genuinely feel that a lot of our social problems today have arisen in large measure because the country led by the government has made an assault on religious convictions. That is fueling a lot of this debate today over what can and cannot be done in the schools.

Much of the tension stems from the idea that religion is simply not welcome at all in what Professor Carter at Yale has called the public square. Americans feel that instead of celebrating their love for God in public, they're being forced to hide their faith behind closed doors. That's wrong. Americans should never have to hide their faith. But some Americans have been denied the right to express their religion and that has to stop. That has happened and it has to stop. It is crucial that government does not dictate or demand specific religious views, but equally crucial that government doesn't prevent the expression of specific religious views.

When the First Amendment is invoked as an obstacle to private expression of religion it is being misused. Religion has a proper place in private and a proper place in public because the public square belongs to all Americans. It's especially important that parents feel confident that their children can practice religion. That's why some families have been frustrated to see their children denied even the most private forms of religious expression in public schools. It is rare, but these things have actually happened.

I know that most schools do a very good job of protecting students' religious rights, but some students in America have been prohibited from reading the Bible silently in study hall. Some student religious groups haven't been allowed to publicize their meetings in the same way that nonreligious groups can. Some students have been prevented even from saying grace before lunch. That is rare, but it has happened and it is wrong. Wherever and whenever the religious rights of children are threatened or suppressed, we must move quickly to correct it. We want to make it easier and more acceptable for people to express and to celebrate their faith.

Now, just because the First Amendment sometimes gets the balance a little bit wrong in specific decisions by specific people doesn't mean there's anything wrong with the First Amendment. I still believe the First Amendment as it is presently written permits the American people to do what they need to do. That's what I believe. (Applause.) Let me give you some examples and you see if you agree.

First of all, the First Amendment does not require students to leave their religion at the schoolhouse door. We wouldn't want students to leave the values they learn from religion, like honesty and sharing and kindness, behind the schoolhouse door—behind at the schoolhouse door, and reinforcing those values is an important part of every school's mission.

Some school officials and teachers and parents believe that the Constitution forbids any religious expression at all in public schools. That is wrong. Our courts have made it clear that that is wrong. It is also not a good idea. Religion is too important to our history and our heritage for us to keep it out of our schools. Once again, it shouldn't be demanded, but as long as it is not sponsored by school officials and doesn't interfere with other children's rights, it mustn't be denied.

For example, students can pray privately and individually whenever they want. They can say grace themselves before lunch. There are times when they can pray out loud together. Student religious clubs in high schools can and should be treated just like any other extracurricular club. They can advertise their meetings, meet on school grounds, use school facilities just as other clubs can. When students can choose to read a book to themselves, they have every right to read the Bible or any other religious text they want.

Teachers can and certainly should teach about religion and the contributions it has made to our history, our values, our knowledge, to our music and our art in our country and around the world, and to the development of the kind of people we are. Students can also pray to themselves—preferably before tests, as I used to do. (Laughter.)

Students should feel free to express their religion and their beliefs in homework, through art work, during class presentations, as long as it's relevant to the assignment. If students can distribute flyers or pamphlets that have nothing to do with the school, they can distribute religious flyers and pamphlets on the same basis. If students can wear T-shirts advertising sports teams, rock groups, or politicians, they can also wear T-shirts that promote religion. If certain subjects or activities are objectionable to their students or their parents because of their religious beliefs, then schools may, and sometimes they must, excuse the students from those activities.

Finally, even though the schools can't advocate religious beliefs, as I said earlier, they should teach mainstream values and virtues. The fact that some of these values happen to be religious values does not mean that they cannot be taught in our schools.

All these forms of religious expression and worship are permitted and protected by the First Amendment. That doesn't change the fact that some students haven't been allowed to express their beliefs in these ways. What we have to do is to work together to help all Americans understand exactly what the First Amendment does. It protects freedom of religion by allowing students to pray, and it protects freedom of religion by preventing schools from telling them how and when and what to pray. The First Amendment keeps us all on common ground. We are allowed to believe and worship as we choose without the government telling any of us what we can and cannot do.

It is in that spirit that I am today directing the Secretary of Education and the Attorney General to provide every school district in America before school starts this fall with a detailed explanation of the religious expression permitted in schools, including all the things that I've talked about today. I hope parents, students, educators, and religious leaders can use this directive as a starting point. I hope it helps them to understand their differences, to protect students' religious rights, and to find common ground. I believe we can find that common ground.

This past April a broad coalition of religious and legal groups—Christian and Jewish, conservative and liberal, Supreme Court advocates and Supreme Court critics—put themselves on the solution side of this debate. They produced a remarkable document called "Religion in Public Schools: A Joint Statement of Current Law." They put aside their deep differences and said, we all agree on what kind of religious expression the law permits in our schools. My directive borrows heavily and gratefully from their wise and thoughtful statement. This is a subject that could have easily divided the men and women that came together to discuss it. But they moved beyond their differences and that may be as important as the specific document they produced.

I also want to mention over 200 religious and civic leaders who signed the Williamsburg Charter in Virginia in 1988. That charter reaffirms the core principles of the First Amendment. We can live together with our deepest differences and all be stronger for it.

The charter signers are impressive in their own right and all the more impressive for their differences of opinion, including Presidents Ford and Carter; Chief Justice Rehnquist and the late Chief Justice Burger; Senator Dole and former Governor Dukakis; Bill Bennett and Lane Kirkland, the president of the AFL-CIO; Norman Lear and Phyllis Schlafly signed it together—(laughter)—Coretta Scott King and Reverend James Dobson.

These people were able to stand up publicly because religion is a personal and private thing for Americans which has to have some public expression. That's how it is for me. I'm pretty old-fashioned about these things. I really do believe in the constancy of sin and the constant possibility of forgiveness, the reality of redemption and the promise of a future life. But I'm also a Baptist who believes that salvation is primarily personal and private, that my relationship is directly with God and not through any intermediary.

People—other people can have different views. And I've spent a good part of my life trying to understand different religious views, celebrate them and figure out what brings us together.

I will say again, the First Amendment is a gift to us. And the Founding Fathers wrote the Constitution in broad ways so that it could grow and change, but hold fast to certain principles. They knew—they knew that all people were fallible and would make mistakes from time to time. And I have—as I said, there are times when the Supreme Court makes a decision, if I disagree with it, one of us is wrong. There's another possibility: both of us could be wrong. (Laughter.) That's the way it is in human affairs.

But what I want to say to the American people and what I want to say to you is that James Madison and Thomas Jefferson did not intend to drive a stake in the heart of religion and to drive it out of our public life. What they intended to do was to set up a system so that we could bring religion into our public life and into our private life without any of us telling the other what to do.

This is a big deal today. One county in America, Los Angeles County, has over 150 different racial and ethnic groups in it—over 150 different. How many religious views do you suppose are in those groups? How many? Every significant religion in the world is represented in significant numbers in one American county, and many smaller religious groups—in one American county.

We have got to get this right. We have got to get this right. And we have to keep this balance. This country needs to be a place where religion grows and flourishes.

Don't you believe that if every kid in every difficult neighborhood in America were in a religious institution on the weekends, the synagogue on Saturday, a church on Sunday, a mosque on Friday, don't you really believe that the drug rate, the crime rate, the violence rate, the sense of self-destruction would go way down and the quality of the character of this country would go way up? (Applause.)

But don't you also believe that if for the last 200 years we had had a state governed religion, people would be bored with it, think that it would—(laughter and applause)—they would think it had been compromised by politicians, shaved around the edges, imposed on people who didn't really consent to it, and we wouldn't have 250,000 houses of worship in America? (Applause.) I mean, we wouldn't.

It may be perfect—imperfect, the First Amendment, but it is the nearest thing ever created in any human society for the promotion of religion and religious values because it left us free to do it. And I strongly believe that the government has made a lot of mistakes which we have tried to roll back in interfering with that around the edges. That's what the Religious Freedom Restoration Act is all about. That's what this directive that Secretary Riley and the Justice Department and I have worked so hard on is all about. That's what our efforts to bring in people of different religious views are all about. And I strongly believe that we have erred when we have rolled it back too much. And I hope that we can have a partnership with our churches in many ways to reach out to the young people who need the values, the hope, the belief, the convictions that comes with faith, and the sense of security in a very uncertain and rapidly changing world.

But keep in mind we have a chance to do it because of the heritage of America and the protection of the First Amendment. We have to get it right.

ACLU Briefing Paper Number 3

This briefing paper, available on the ACLU's web site, answers a number of common questions about religion in the schools and also states the ACLU's position on the issue of religion in the schools. Although the ACLU is correctly regarded as supporting a "strict separationist" view, the answers in this briefing paper supply an accurate statement of current law. The briefing paper clearly articulates when a statement is a "position" of the organization.

Church and State

The United States is the most religiously diverse nation in the world. More than 1,500 different religious bodies and sects, including 75 varieties of Baptists alone, co-exist and flourish in our nation. We have 360,000 churches, mosques, and synagogues.

Americans are also extremely devout. According to recent surveys, more than 90 percent of Americans profess a belief in God; more than half say they pray at least once a day, and more than 40 percent say they have attended worship services during the previous week. The Census Bureau reports that 63 percent of the population claims church membership, a figure that has remained virtually unchanged since the 1960 census.

How has the U.S. been able to maintain, on the one hand, an extremely diverse and devout religious population, and on the other an extremely low incidence of sectarian strife? The American Civil Liberties Union believes that the answer lies in a time-tested formula: the complete separation of church and state required by the First Amendment to our Constitution.

Many people mistakenly believe that separation of church and state implies official hostility to religion. But, in fact, the opposite is true: It was their belief in the preciousness and sanctity of religious faith that engendered the Founders' determination to protect religion from government interference. They understood that religious liberty can flourish only if the government leaves religion alone.

For more than 75 years, the ACLU has defended religious freedom and challenged attempts by sectarians to impose their religious beliefs and practices on others through government sponsorship.

In 1925, the ACLU defended biology teacher John Scopes, in the famous "monkey trial," against the charge that he had broken Tennessee's fundamentalist-inspired ban on the teaching of evolution.

In the 1930s, the ACLU supported the right of Jehovah's Witness schoolchildren not to salute the American flag, which would have violated their religious beliefs.

In 1947, the ACLU participated in the landmark case, *Everson v. Board of Education,* in which the United States Supreme Court proclaimed:

> The First Amendment has erected a wall of separation between church and state. That wall must be kept

high and impregnable. We would not approve the slightest breach.

In the 1950s and 1960s, responding to numerous complaints from the public, the ACLU challenged official prayer and Bible reading in the nation's public schools—and won. the Supreme Court ruled, in *Engel v. Vitale* and in *School District of Abington Township v. Schempp,* that school prayer and Bible reading are unconstitutional.

In the 1980s, the ACLU successfully fought bills introduced in 23 state legislatures mandating that the public schools teach "scientific creationism"—the biblical version of the earth's creation.

In the early 1990s, the ACLU joined with religious and civil liberties organizations to fight for Congressional passage of the Religious Freedom Restoration Act, which strengthens protection for the rights of religious minorities.

Today, as in the past, the main arena of struggle is in the nation's public schools. And today, as in the past, the ACLU offers legal assistance to parents, students, teachers, school board members and school administrators in resisting the efforts of religious groups to impose devotional activities in the classroom, on sports fields and at graduation exercises.

Religion and American Public Schools: The History of Prayer in Our Public Schools

The controversy over officially sponsored prayer in public schools did not begin in 1962, when the Supreme Court first ruled that such observances violate the Establishment Clause. It began more than 100 years earlier, in the 1830s, when waves of Italian and Irish Catholic immigrants came to this country and objected to compulsory readings of the Protestant King James Bible and the recitation of Protestant prayers in most public schools. A bitter conflict erupted, including riots, the expulsion of Catholic children from public schools, the burning of convents and even some deaths.

In the 1950s, as the religious diversity of our society increased, school prayer became a divisive issue once again. Now Jewish, Buddhist, Hindu, Moslem and atheist parents objected to Christian practices in the public schools.

Out of this conflict arose *Engel v. Vitale,* a 1962 case in which the Supreme Court ruled against officially sponsored and organized school prayer: "We think," wrote Justice Hugo L. Black for the Court, "that by using its public school system to encourage recitation of the Regents' prayer [a nondenominational prayer created by the government], the State of New York has adopted a practice wholly inconsistent with the Establishment Clause." The following year, in *School District of Abington Township v. Schempp,* the Court held that Bible readings in public schools also violate the First Amendment.

President John F. Kennedy, the country's first Catholic president, urged respect for the Court's decision in *Engel:*

> We have in this case a very easy remedy, and that is to pray ourselves. And I would think it would be a welcome reminder to every American family that we can pray a good deal more at home, we can attend our churches with a good deal more fidelity, and we can make the true meaning of prayer much more important in the lives of our children.

But not everyone agreed with the president. Within a month, over 25 resolutions, calling for constitutional amendments to override the Court's decision, were introduced in Congress—including one that urged adoption of a "Christian amendment." Organized efforts to circumvent the *Engel* ruling have continued ever since, and schools and school districts throughout the country have continued to sponsor prayer in violation of the rights of religious minorities.

• What's wrong with official school prayer?

Officially organized and sponsored devotional exercises in the public school setting are inconsistent with the principle of religious liberty in several ways. Such exercises make children feel they must participate or face the disdain of their teachers and fellow students. Children whose religious beliefs are different from those of the majority must not be made to feel like outsiders in their schools.

Official school prayer also usurps the right of parents to determine if, how, when, where and to whom their children should pray. When schools sponsor prayer or any other religious activity, they infringe on parents' right to choose the religious tradition in which they raise their children. Muslim, Jewish or Hindu parents don't want their children to participate in Christian observances. Atheist parents don't want their children to pray at all. Parents should not have to fear that the public schools are indoctrinating their children in beliefs that are counter to their families' beliefs.

• Can students ever pray in school?

Of course. Religious speech, like other speech, is protected by the First Amendment. Public school students have the right to read the Bible, recite the rosary, pray before meals and examinations and discuss their religious views with their fellow students, as long as they do so outside of the educational process.

Students do not, however, have the right to impose their religious expression on a captive audience of other students—for example, by broadcasting religious pronouncements or prayers over the school public address system—nor to compel other students to engage in any religious activity.

• What about "student-initiated" prayer?

The issue of "student-initiated prayer" has arisen in the context of graduation ceremonies. Until 1992, it was common in some parts of the country for a member of the clergy to offer a prayer during graduation exercises. But that year, the Supreme Court ruled in Lee v. Weisman that including prayer in a school-sponsored and -supervised graduation ceremony violated the Establishment Clause. Justice Anthony P. Kennedy, writing for the Court, explained:

> The prayer exercises in this case are especially improper because the State has in every practical sense compelled attendance and participation in an explicitly religious exercise at an event of singular importance to every student, one the objecting student had no real alternative to avoid.

As with the *Engel* decision 30 years earlier, an outcry from certain religious quarters greeted the Weisman ruling. Seizing upon what they viewed as a loophole, some religious leaders argued that though the Court had prohibited clergy from delivering prayer at graduations, it had not barred students from doing so. "Student-initiated prayer" must be allowed, they said. Some school administrators and school boards proceeded to allow graduating classes to vote on whether or not a student volunteer would deliver a prayer at graduation. This led to another round of lawsuits by students and parents opposed to any form of organized prayer at graduations. The Supreme Court has not yet ruled in this latest struggle.

The ACLU believes that the Court's ruling in Weisman is as crystal clear in prohibiting "student-initiated prayer" as it is in barring prayer by members of the clergy. Why? Because a graduation ceremony is a public school event. Time for prayer at that event can be reserved only with the school administration's consent. Thus, no matter who initiates the prayer, whether students, teachers or parents, school officials presiding at that school event are the prayer's sponsors—which violates the Establishment Clause.

As for the claim that students should be free to vote a prayer up or down, that directly infringes on the fundamental constitutional rights of students and parents who belong to minority religions. Fundamental rights, being inalienable, are not subject to a vote. Justice Robert H. Jackson best explained this principle in his 1943 opinion recognizing the right of Jehovah's Witnesses not to salute the flag:

> The very purpose of a Bill of Rights was to withdraw certain subjects from the vicissitudes of political controversy, to place them beyond the reach of majorities and officials and to establish them as legal principles to be applied by the courts. One's right to life, liberty and property, to free speech, a free press, freedom of worship and assembly, and other fundamental rights may not be submitted to vote; they depend on the outcome of no elections. (*West Virginia v. Barnette*)

• But wouldn't prayer in school help restore moral values to our classrooms?

Concern that a crisis of values exists in our society is widespread in the face of violent crime, troubled and disintegrating families, and many young people's seeming hopelessness and lack of direction. Many Americans look to religion as the primary source of values and urge a stronger role for religion in public life.

Prayer and perhaps other religious observances, they argue, would be an antidote to today's social problems. Some even contend that a steep moral decline in the nation was caused mainly by the removal of organized prayer from the schools in accordance with the 1962 Supreme Court decision in *Engel v. Vitale*. These viewpoints are problematic on several counts:

• It is simplistic to think that mere recitation of a necessarily watered down, nondenominational prayer every morning could have any impact on complicated social problems that are rooted in poverty, inequality and lack of opportunity.

• If removal of organized prayer from the schools caused the alleged "decline in moral values," how is it that Americans are as religious today as ever?

• Nostalgia for a presumably "moral" United States of the past ignores the reality that before 1962 organized school prayer coexisted with Jim Crow laws in the South, official discrimination against women in education and employment, and political repression in public life. If anything, our nation is a more moral place today given the vigorous attempts to eradicate bigotry from our political, cultural and social institutions.

Public schools do and should impart moral values to our children, including the civic virtues of honesty, good citizenship, ethics and respect for the rights and freedoms of others. But religion should be practiced in the home, the church, the synagogue, the temple and the mosque and not at official events.

• Do student clubs have the right to use school facilities?

Yes. The Equal Access Act, passed by Congress in 1984, protects the right of secondary school students to hold religious club meetings on public school grounds during noninstructional time, if other, noncurriculum-related student groups—such as political clubs, community service clubs, etc.—are also allowed to meet at a school. The Supreme Court upheld the constitutionality of the Act in 1990, in *Westside Community Schools v. Mergens*. The Court indicated, however, that schools must treat religious clubs differently from other student clubs. To guard against improper governmental support for religion, school employees may not initiate, direct or participate in religious club meetings—although a school staff person may be present to keep order and ensure safety.

Teaching about Evolution and the Nature of Science

The following document is an excerpt from the National Academy of Science's document "Teaching About Evolution and the Nature of Science." This document provides three statements on the teaching of evolution in the schools from the National Science Teachers Association, the National Association of Biology Teachers, and the American Association for the Advancement of Science Commission on Science Education, respectively.

A NSTA (National Science Teachers Association) Position Statement on the Teaching of Evolution[1] Approved by the NSTA Board of Directors, July 1997

Introductory Remarks

The National Science Teachers Association supports the position that evolution is a major unifying concept of science and should be included as part of K–College science frameworks and curricula. NSTA recognizes that evolution has not been emphasized in science curricula in a manner commensurate to its importance because of official policies, intimidation of science teachers, the general public's misunderstanding of evolutionary theory, and a century of controversy.

Furthermore, teachers are being pressured to introduce creationism, creation "science," and other nonscientific views, which are intended to weaken or eliminate the teaching of evolution.

Within this context, NSTA recommends that:

• Science curricula and teachers should emphasize evolution in a manner commensurate with its importance as a unifying concept in science and its overall explanatory power.

• Policymakers and administrators should not mandate policies requiring the teaching of creation science or related concepts such as so-called "intelligent design," "abrupt appearance," and "arguments against evolution."

• Science teachers should not advocate any religious view about creation, nor advocate the converse: that there is no possibility of supernatural influence in bringing about the universe as we know it. Teachers should be nonjudgmental about the personal beliefs of students.

• Administrators should provide support to teachers as they design and implement curricula that emphasize evolution. This should include inservice education to assist teachers to teach evolution in a comprehensive and professional manner. Administrators also should support teachers against pressure to promote nonscientific views or to diminish or eliminate the study of evolution.

• Parental and community involvement in establishing the goals of science education and the curriculum development process should be encouraged and nurtured in our democratic society. However, the professional responsibility of science teachers and curriculum specialists to provide students with quality science education should not be bound by censorship, pseudoscience, inconsistencies, faulty scholarship, or unconstitutional mandates.

• Science textbooks shall emphasize evolution as a unifying concept. Publishers should not be required or volunteer to include disclaimers in textbooks concerning the nature and study of evolution.

NSTA offers the following background information:

The Nature of Science and Scientific Theories

Science is a method of explaining the natural world. It assumes the universe operates according to regularities and that through systematic investigation we can understand these regularities. The methodology of science emphasizes the logical testing of alternate explanations of natural phenomena against empirical data. Because science is limited to explaining the natural world by means of natural processes, it cannot use supernatural causation in its explanations. Similarly, science is precluded from making statements about supernatural forces because these are outside its provenance. Science has increased our knowledge because of this insistence on the search for natural causes.

The most important scientific explanations are called "theories." In ordinary speech, "theory" is often used to mean "guess," or "hunch," whereas in scientific terminology, a theory is a set of universal statements which explain the natural world. Theories are powerful tools. Scientists seek to develop theories that

- are internally consistent and compatible with the evidence
- are firmly grounded in and based upon evidence
- have been tested against a diverse range of phenomena
- possess broad and demonstrable effectiveness in problem solving
- explain a wide variety of phenomena.

The body of scientific knowledge changes as new observations and discoveries are made. Theories and other explanations change. New theories emerge and other theories are modified or discarded. Throughout this process, theories are formulated and tested on the basis of evidence, internal consistency, and their explanatory power.

Evolution as a Unifying Concept

Evolution in the broadest sense can be defined as the idea that the universe has a history: that change through time has taken place. If we look today at the galaxies, stars, the planet earth, and the life on planet earth, we see that things today are different from what they were in the past: galaxies, stars, planets, and life forms have evolved. Biological evolution refers to the scientific theory that living things share ancestors from which they have diverged: Darwin called it "descent with modification." There is abundant and consistent evidence from astronomy, physics, biochemistry, geochronology, geology, biology, anthropology, and other sciences that evolution has taken place.

As such, evolution is a unifying concept for science. The National Science Education Standards recognizes that conceptual schemes such as evolution "unify science disciplines and provide students with powerful ideas to help them understand the natural world," and recommends evolution as one such scheme. In addition, the Benchmarks for Science Literacy from the American Association for the Advancement of Science's Project 2061 and NSTA's Scope, Sequence, and Coordination Project, as well as other national calls for science reform, all name evolution as a unifying concept because of its importance across the discipline of science. Scientific disciplines with a historical component, such as astronomy, geology, biology, and anthropology, cannot be taught with integrity if evolution is not emphasized.

There is no longer a debate among scientists over whether evolution has taken place. There is considerable debate about how evolution has taken place: the processes and mechanisms producing change, and what has happened during the history of the universe. Scientists often disagree about their explanations. In any science, disagreements are subject to rules of evaluation. Errors and false conclusions are confronted by experiment and observation, and evolution, as in any aspect of science, is continually open to and subject to experimentation and questioning.

Creationism

The word "creationism" has many meanings. In its broadest meaning, creationism is the idea that a supernatural power or powers created. Thus to Christians, Jews, and Muslims, God created; to the Navajo, the Hero Twins created. In a narrower sense, "creationism" has come to mean "special creation": the doctrine that the universe and all that is in it was created by God in essentially its present form, at one time. The most common variety of special creationism asserts that

- the earth is very young
- life was originated by a creator
- life appeared suddenly
- kinds of organisms have not changed
- all life was designed for certain functions and purposes.

This version of special creation is derived from a literal interpretation of Biblical Genesis. It is a specific, sectarian religious belief that is not held by all religious people. Many Christians and Jews believe that God created through the process of evolution. Pope John Paul II, for example, issued a statement in 1996 that reiterated the Catholic position that God created, but that the scientific evidence for evolution is strong.

"Creation science" is an effort to support special creationism through methods of science. Teachers are often pressured to include it or synonyms such as "intelligent design theory," "abrupt appearance theory," "initial complexity theory," or "arguments against evolution" when they teach evolution. Special creationist claims have been discredited by the available evidence. They have no power to explain the natural world and its diverse phenomena. Instead, creationists seek out supposed anomalies among many existing theories and accepted facts. Furthermore, creation science claims do not provide a basis for solving old or new problems or for acquiring new information.

Nevertheless, as noted in the National Science Education Standards, explanations on how the natural world changed based on myths, personal beliefs, religious values, mystical inspiration, superstition, or authority may be personally useful and socially relevant, but they are not scientific. Because science can only use natural explanations and not supernatural ones, science teachers should not advocate any religious view about creation, nor advocate the converse: that there is no possibility of supernatural influence in bringing about the universe as we know it.

Legal Issues

Several judicial rulings have clarified issues surrounding the teaching of evolution and the imposition of mandates that creation science be taught when evolution is taught. The First Amendment of the Constitution requires that public institutions such as schools be religiously neutral; because special creation is a specific, sectarian religious view, it cannot be advocated as "true," accurate scholarship in the public schools. When Arkansas passed a law requiring "equal time" for creationism and evolution, the law was challenged in Federal District Court. Opponents of the bill included the religious leaders of the United Methodist, Episcopalian, Roman Catholic, African Methodist Episcopal, Presbyterian, and Southern Baptist churches, and several educational organizations. After a full trial, the judge ruled that creation science did not qualify as a scientific theory (*McLean v. Arkansas Board of Education*, 529 F. Supp. 1255 [ED Ark. 1982]).

Louisiana's equal time law was challenged in court and eventually reached the Supreme Court. In *Edwards v. Aguillard* 482 U.S. 578 (1987), the Court determined that creationism was inherently a religious idea and to mandate or advocate it in the public schools would be unconstitutional. Other court decisions have upheld the right of a district to require that a teacher teach evolution and not teach creation science: (*Webster v. New Lennox School District* #122, 917 F.2d 1003 [7th Cir. 1990]; *Peloza v. Capistrano Unified School District*, 37 F.3d 517 [9th Cir. 1994]).

Some legislatures and policymakers continue attempts to distort the teaching of evolution through mandates that would require teachers to teach evolution as "only a theory," or that require a textbook or lesson on evolution to be preceded by a disclaimer. Regardless of the legal status of these mandates, they are bad educational policy. Such policies have the effect of intimidating teachers, which may result in the de-emphasis or omission of evolution. The public will only be further confused about the special nature of scientific theories, and if less evolution is learned by students, science literacy itself will suffer.

References

American Association for the Advancement of Science (AAAS). 1993. *Benchmarks for Science Literacy*. Project 2061. New York: Oxford University Press.

Daniel v. Waters. 515 F.2d 485 (6th Cir., 1975).

Edwards v. Aguillard. 482 U.S. 578 (1987).

Epperson v. Arkansas. 393 U.S. 97 (1968).

Laudan, Larry. 1996. *Beyond Positivism and Relativism: Theory, Method, and Evidence*. Boulder, CO: Westview Press.

McLean v. Arkansas Board of Education. 529 F. Supp. 1255 (D. Ark. 1982).

National Research Council (NRC). 1996. *National Science Education Standards*. Washington, DC: National Academy Press.

National Science Teachers Association. 1993. *The Content Core: Vol. I*. Rev. ed. Arlington, VA: National Science Teachers Association.

NSTA. 1996. *A Framework for High School Science Education.* Arlington, VA: National Science Teachers Association.

Peloza v. Capistrano Unified School District. 37 F.3d 517 (9th Cir. 1994).

Ruse, Michael. 1996. *But Is It Science? The Philosophical Question in the Creation/Evolution Controversy.* Amherst, NY: Prometheus Books.

Webster v. New Lennox School District #122. 917 F.2d 1003 (7th Cir. 1990).

Task Force Members

Gerald Skoog, Chair, College of Education, Texas Tech University, Lubbock, Texas

Randy Cielen, Joseph Teres School, Winnipeg, Manitoba, Canada

Linda Jordan, Science Consultant, Franklin, Tennessee

Janis Lariviere, Westlake Alternative Learning Center, Austin, Texas

Larry Scharmann, Kansas State University, Manhattan, Kansas

Eugenie Scott, National Center for Science Education, Berkeley, California

2. National Association of Biology Teachers Statement on Teaching Evolution[2]

As stated in *The American Biology Teacher* by the eminent scientist Theodosius Dobzhansky (1973), "Nothing in biology makes sense except in the light of evolution."[3] This often-quoted assertion accurately illuminates the central, unifying role of evolution in nature, and therefore in biology. Teaching biology in an effective and scientifically-honest manner requires classroom discussions and laboratory experiences on evolution.

Modern biologists constantly study, ponder and deliberate the patterns, mechanisms and pace of evolution, but they do not debate evolution's occurrence. The fossil record and the diversity of extant organisms, combined with modern techniques of molecular biology, taxonomy and geology, provide exhaustive examples and powerful evidence for genetic variation, natural selection, speciation, extinction and other well-established components of current evolutionary theory. Scientific deliberations and modifications of these components clearly demonstrate the vitality and scientific integrity of evolution and the theory that explains it.

The same examination, pondering and possible revision have firmly established evolution as an important natural process explained by valid scientific principles, and clearly differentiate and separate science from various kinds of nonscientific ways of knowing, including those with a supernatural basis such as creationism. Whether called "creation science," "scientific creationism," "intelligent-design theory," "young-earth theory" or some other synonym, creation beliefs have no place in the science classroom. Explanations employing nonnaturalistic or supernatural events, whether or not explicit reference is made to a supernatural being, are outside the realm of science and not part of a valid science curriculum. Evolutionary theory, indeed all of science, is necessarily silent on religion and neither refutes nor supports the existence of a deity or deities.

Accordingly, the National Association of Biology Teachers, an organization of science teachers, endorses the following tenets of science, evolution and biology education:

- The diversity of life on earth is the outcome of evolution: an unpredictable and natural process of temporal descent with genetic modification that is affected by natural selection, chance, historical contingencies and changing environments.

- Evolutionary theory is significant in biology, among other reasons, for its unifying properties and predictive features, the clear empirical testability of its integral models, and the richness of new scientific research it fosters.

- The fossil record, which includes abundant transitional forms in diverse taxonomic groups, establishes extensive and comprehensive evidence for organic evolution.

- Natural selection, the primary mechanism for evolutionary changes, can be demonstrated with numerous, convincing examples, both extant and extinct.

- Natural selection—a differential, greater survival and reproduction of some genetic variants within a population under an existing environmental state—has no specific direction or goal, including survival of a species.

- Adaptations do not always provide an obvious selective advantage. Furthermore, there is no indication that adaptations—molecular to organismal—must be perfect: adaptations providing a selective advantage must simply be good enough for survival and increased reproductive fitness.

- The model of punctuated equilibrium provides another

account of the tempo of speciation in the fossil record of many lineages: it does not refute or overturn evolutionary theory, but instead adds to its scientific richness.

• Evolution does not violate the second law of thermodynamics: producing order from disorder is possible with the addition of energy, such as from the sun.

• Although comprehending deep time is difficult, the earth is about 4.5 billion years old. Homo sapiens has occupied only a minuscule moment of that immense duration of time.

• When compared with earlier periods, the Cambrian explosion evident in the fossil record reflects at least three phenomena: the evolution of animals with readily fossilized hard body parts; Cambrian environment (sedimentary rock) more conducive to preserving fossils; and the evolution from pre-Cambrian forms of an increased diversity of body patterns in animals.

• Radiometric and other dating techniques, when used properly, are highly accurate means of establishing dates in the history of the planet and in the history of life.

• In science, a theory is not a guess or an approximation but an extensive explanation developed from well-documented, reproducible sets of experimentally-derived data from repeated observations of natural processes.

• The models and the subsequent outcomes of a scientific theory are not decided in advance, but can be, and often are, modified and improved as new empirical evidence is uncovered. Thus, science is a constantly self-correcting endeavor to understand nature and natural phenomena.

• Science is not teleological: the accepted processes do not start with a conclusion, then refuse to change it, or acknowledge as valid only those data that support an unyielding conclusion. Science does not base theories on an untestable collection of dogmatic proposals. Instead, the processes of science are characterized by asking questions, proposing hypotheses, and designing empirical models and conceptual frameworks for research about natural events.

• Providing a rational, coherent and scientific account of the taxonomic history and diversity of organisms requires inclusion of the mechanisms and principles of evolution.

• Similarly, effective teaching of cellular and molecular biology requires inclusion of evolution.

• Specific textbook chapters on evolution should be included in biology curricula, and evolution should be a recurrent theme throughout biology textbooks and courses.

• Students can maintain their religious beliefs and learn the scientific foundations of evolution.

• Teachers should respect diverse beliefs, but contrasting science with religion, such as belief in creationism, is not a role of science. Science teachers can, and often do, hold devout religious beliefs, accept evolution as a valid scientific theory, and teach the theory's mechanisms and principles.

• Science and religion differ in significant ways that make it inappropriate to teach any of the different religious beliefs in the science classroom.

• Opposition to teaching evolution reflects confusion about the nature and processes of science. Teachers can, and should, stand firm and teach good science with the acknowledged support of the courts. In *Epperson v. Arkansas* (1968), the U.S. Supreme Court struck down a 1928 Arkansas law prohibiting the teaching of evolution in state schools. In *McLean v. Arkansas* (1982), the federal district court invalidated a state statute requiring equal classroom time for evolution and creationism.

Edwards v. Aguillard (1987) led to another Supreme Court ruling against so-called "balanced treatment" of creation science and evolution in public schools. In this landmark case, the Court called the Louisiana equal-time statute "facially invalid as violative of the Establishment Clause of the First Amendment, because it lacks a clear secular purpose." This decision— "the *Edwards* restriction"—is now the controlling legal position on attempts to mandate the teaching of creationism: the nation's highest court has said that such mandates are unconstitutional. Subsequent district court decisions in Illinois and California have applied "the *Edwards* restriction" to teachers who advocate creation science, and to the right of a district to prohibit an individual teacher from promoting creation science, in the classroom.

Courts have thus restricted school districts from requiring creation science in the science curriculum and have restricted individual instructors from teaching it. All teachers and administrators should be mindful of these court cases, remembering that the law, science and NABT support them as they appropriately include the teaching of evolution in the science curriculum.

References and Suggested Reading

Clough, M. 1994. "Diminish students' resistance to biological evolution." *American Biology Teacher* 56(Oct.):409-415.

Futuyma, D. 1997. *Evolutionary Biology.* 3rd ed. Sunderland, MA: Sinauer Associates, Inc.

Gillis, A. 1994. "Keeping creationism out of the classroom." *BioScience* 44:650-656.

Gould, S. 1977. *Ever Since Darwin: Reflections in Natural History.* New York: W.W. Norton.

Gould, S. 1994. "The evolution of life on the earth." *Scientific American* 271(Oct.):85-91.

Mayr, E. 1991. *One Long Argument: Charles Darwin and the Genesis of Modern Evolutionary Thought.* Cambridge, MA: Harvard University Press.

McComas, W., ed. 1994. *Investigating Evolutionary Biology in the Laboratory.* Reston, VA: National Association of Biology Teachers.

Moore, J. 1993. *Science as a Way of Knowing: The Foundation of Modern Biology.* Cambridge, MA: Harvard University Press.

National Center for Science Education, P.O. Box 9477, Berkeley, CA 94709. Numerous publications such as "Facts, faith and fairness: Scientific creationism clouds scientific literacy" by S. Walsh and T. Demere.

Numbers, R. 1993. *The Creationists: The Evolution of Scientific Creationism.* Berkeley, CA: University of California Press.

Weiner, J. 1994. *The Beak of the Finch: A Story of Evolution in Our Time.* New York: Alfred A. Knopf.

3. Resolution passed by the American Association for the Advancement of Science Commission on Science Education[4]

The Commission on Science Education of the American Association for the Advancement of Science, is vigorously opposed to attempts by some boards of education, and other groups, to require that religious accounts of creation be taught in science classes.

During the past century and a half, the earth's crust and the fossils preserved in it have been intensively studied by geologists and paleontologists. Biologists have intensively studied the origin, structure, physiology, and genetics of living organisms. The conclusion of these studies is that the living species of animals and plants have evolved from different species that lived in the past. The scientists involved in these studies have built up the body of knowledge known as the biological theory of the origin and evolution of life. There is no currently acceptable alternative scientific theory to explain the phenomena.

The various accounts of creation that are part of the religious heritage of many people are not scientific statements or theories. They are statements that one may choose to believe, but if he does, this is a matter of faith, because such statements are not subject to study or verification by the procedures of science. A scientific statement must be capable of test by observation and experiment. It is acceptable only if, after repeated testing, it is found to account satisfactorily for the phenomena to which it is applied.

Thus the statements about creation that are part of many religions have no place in the domain of science and should not be regarded as reasonable alternatives to scientific explanations for the origin and evolution of life.

Resolution on Inclusion of the Theory of Creation in Science Curricula[5]

WHEREAS some State Boards of Education and State Legislatures have required or are considering requiring inclusion of the theory of creation as an alternative to evolutionary theory in discussions of origins of life, and

WHEREAS the requirement that the theory of creation be included in textbooks as an alternative to evolutionary theory represents a constraint upon the freedom of the science teacher in the classroom, and

WHEREAS its inclusion also represents dictation by a lay body of what shall be considered within the corpus of a science,

THEREFORE the American Association for the Advancement of Science strongly urges that reference to the theory of creation, which is neither scientifically grounded nor capable of performing the roles required of scientific theories, not be required in textbooks and other classroom materials intended for use in science curricula.

Statement on Forced Teaching of Creationist Beliefs in Public School Science Education[6]

WHEREAS it is the responsibility of the American Association for the Advancement of Science to preserve the integrity of science, and

WHEREAS science is a systematic method of investigation based on continuous experimentation, observation, and measurement leading to evolving explanations of natural phenomena, explanations which are continuously open to further testing, and

WHEREAS evolution fully satisfies these criteria, irrespective of remaining debates concerning its detailed mechanisms, and

WHEREAS the Association respects the right of people to hold diverse beliefs about creation that do not come within the definitions of science, and

WHEREAS creationist groups are imposing beliefs disguised as science upon teachers and students to the detriment and distortion of public education in the United States,

THEREFORE be it resolved that because "creationist science" has no scientific validity it should not be taught as science, and further, that the AAAS views legislation requiring "creationist science" to be taught in public schools as a real and present threat to the integrity of education and the teaching of science, and

Be it further resolved that the AAAS urges citizens, educational authorities, and legislators to oppose the compulsory inclusion in science education curricula of beliefs that are not amenable to the process of scrutiny, testing, and revision that is indispensable to science.

Notes

1. Reprinted with permission from NSTA Publications, copyright 1997 from NSTA Handbook, 1997-1998, National Science Teachers Association, 1840 Wilson Boulevard, Arlington, VA 22201-3000.

2. Statement on Teaching Evolution, National Association of Biology Teachers (NABT). Adopted by the NABT Board of Directors on March 15, 1995.

3. Dobzhansky, T. 1973. Nothing in biology makes sense except in the light of evolution. American Biology Teacher 35:125-129.

4. American Association for the Advancement of Science (AAAS), Commission on Science Education. October 13, 1972.

5. Adopted by AAAS Council on December 30, 1972.

6. Adopted by the AAAS Board of Directors on January 4, 1982, and by the AAAS Council on January 7, 1982.

Proposed Constitutional Amendments

Over the years a number of constitutional amendments have been proposed to interpret the religion clauses in the U.S. Constitution's First Amendment. Currently, the emphasis is on amending the U.S. Constitution specifically to allow organized prayer and other religious activity in the public schools. The following are a sample of the proposed amendments concerning religion in the schools.

Proposed Blaine Amendment (1876)

[Although the amendment passed the House of Representatives, it failed to receive the needed two-third's vote in the Senate and was never forwarded to the states for ratification.]

No state shall make any law respecting the establishment of religion or prohibiting the free exercise thereof; and no religious test shall ever be required as a qualification to any office or public trust under any state. No public property, and no public revenue of, nor any loan of credit by or under the authority of the United States or any state, territory, District, or municipal corporation, shall be appropriated to, or used for, the support of any school, educational, or other institution, under the control of any religious or anti-religious sect, organization, or denomination, or wherein the particular creed or tenets of any religious or anti-religious sect, organization, or denomination, or wherein the particular creed or tenets of any religious sect, organization, or denomination be taught. And no such particular creed or tenets shall be read or taught in any school or institution supported in whole or in part by such revenue or loan of credit; and no such appropriation or loan of credit shall be made to any religious or anti-religious sect, organization or denomination, or to promote its interests or tenets. This article shall not be construed to prohibit the reading of the Bible in any school or institution; and it shall not have the effect to impair rights of property already invested.

Proposed Prayer Amendment (1992)

Nothing in this Constitution shall be construed to prohibit individual or group prayer in public schools or other public institutions. No person shall be required by the United States or by any State to participate in prayer. Neither the United States nor any State shall compose the words of any prayer to be said in public schools.

Proposed Religious Equality Amendment (1994)

Section 1. Neither the United States nor any State shall abridge the freedom of any person or group, including students in public schools, to engage in prayer or other religious expression in circumstances in which expression of a nonreligious character would be permitted; nor deny benefits to or otherwise discriminate against any person or group on account of the religious character of their speech, ideas, motivations or identity.

Section 2. Nothing in the Constitution shall be construed to forbid the United States or any State to give public or ceremonial acknowledgement to the religious heritage, beliefs, or traditions of its people.

Section 3. The exercise, by the people, of any freedoms under the First Amendment or under this Amendment shall not constitute an establishment of religion.

Proposed Religious Freedom Amendment (1997)

To secure the people's right to acknowledge God according to the dictates of conscience: The people's right to pray and to recognize their religious beliefs, heritage or traditions on public property, including schools, shall not be infringed. The government shall not require any person to join in prayer or other religious activity, initiate or designate school prayers, discriminate against religion, or deny equal access to a benefit on account of religion.

Arkansas Anti-Evolution Statute

During the first half of the twentieth century several states enacted laws banning the teaching of evolution in both public schools and universities. Religious individuals and groups object to the teaching of evolution because it runs counter to the literal explanation in the Bible. The famous Scopes Monkey Trial upheld Tennessee's antievolution statute in 1925. One by one these laws were challenged and declared invalid and an impermissible intrusion of religion in the schools. In 1947 the Arkansas Supreme Court upheld the following statute. The U.S. Supreme Court, however, overruled the Arkansas Court and ruled the statute unconstitutional in *Epperson v. Arkansas* (1968).

Arkansas Statutes Annotated 1947, paragraphs 80–1627, 80–1628

80–1627. Doctrine of ascent or descent of man from lower order of animals prohibited. It shall be unlawful for any teacher or other instructor in any University, College, Normal, Public School, or other institution of the State, which is supported in whole or in part from public funds derived by State and local taxation to teach the theory or doctrine that mankind ascended or descended from a lower order of animals and also shall it be unlawful for any teacher, textbook commission, or other authority exercising the power to select textbooks for above mentioned educational institutions to adopt or use in any such institutions a textbook that teaches the doctrine or theory that mankind descended or ascended from a lower order of animals.

80–1628. Teaching doctrine or adopting textbooks mentioning doctrine—Penalties—Positions to be vacated. Any teacher or other instructor or textbook commissioner who is found guilty of violation of this act by teaching the theory or doctrine mentioned in section 1 hereof, or by using, or adopting any such textbooks in any such educational institution shall be guilty of a misdemeanor and upon conviction shall be fined not exceeding five hundred dollars ($500.00); and upon conviction shall vacate the position thus held in any educational institutions of the character above mentioned or any commission of which he may be a member.

Court Cases

Everson v. Board of Education of the Township of Ewing, 330 U.S. 1 (1947)

Mr. Justice Black delivered the opinion of the Court.

. . . [The] township board of education, acting pursuant to this statute, authorized reimbursement to parents of money expended by them for the bus transportation of their children on regular buses operated by the public transportation system. Part of this money was for the payment of transportation of some children in the community to Catholic parochial schools. These church schools give their students, in addition to secular education, regular religious instruction conforming to the religious tenets and modes of worship of the Catholic Faith. The superintendent of these schools is a Catholic priest.

The appellant, in his capacity as a district taxpayer, filed suit in a state court challenging the right of the Board to reimburse parents of parochial school students. He contended that the statute and the resolution passed pursuant to it violated both the State and the Federal Constitutions.

[The trial courts found the law unconstitutional, but the state court of appeals reversed and the case was appealed to the U.S. Supreme Court.]

. . . The "establishment of religion" clause of the First Amendment means at least this: neither a state nor the Federal Government can set up a church. Neither can pass laws which aid one religion, aid all religions, or prefer one religion over another. Neither can force nor influence a person to go to or to remain away from church against his will or force him to profess a belief or disbelief in any religion. No person can be punished for entertaining or professing religious beliefs or disbeliefs, for church attendance or non-attendance. No tax in any amount, large or small, can be levied to support any religious activities or institutions, whatever they may be called, or whatever form they may adopt to teach or practice religion. Neither a state nor the Federal Government can, openly or secretly, participate in the affairs of any religious organizations or groups, and vice versa. In the words of Jefferson, the clause against establishment of religion by law was intended to erect "a wall of separation between church and State."

. . . We cannot say that the First Amendment prohibits New Jersey from spending tax-raised funds to pay the bus fares of parochial school pupils as a part of a general program under which it pays the fares of pupils attending public and other schools. It is undoubtedly true that children are helped to get to church schools. There is even a possibility that some of the children might not be sent to the church schools if the parents were compelled to pay their children's bus fares out of their own pockets when transportation to a public school would have been paid for by the State. The same possibility exists where the state requires a local transit company to provide reduced fares to school children, including those attending parochial schools, or where a municipally owned transportation system undertakes to carry all school children free of charge. Moreover, state-paid policemen, detailed to protect children going to and from church schools from the very real hazards of traffic, would serve much the same purpose and accomplish much the same result as state provisions intended to guarantee free transportation of a kind which the state deems to be best for the school children's welfare. And parents might refuse to risk their children to the serious danger of traffic accidents going to and from parochial schools the approaches to which were not protected by policemen. Similarly, parents might be reluctant to permit their children to attend schools which the state had cut off from such general government services as ordinary police and fire protection, connections for sewage disposal, public highways and sidewalks. Of course, cutting off church schools from these services so separate and so indisputably marked off from the religious function would make it far more difficult for the schools to operate. But such is obviously not the purpose of the First Amendment. That Amendment requires the state to be neutral in its relations with groups of religious believers and nonbelievers; it does not require the state to be their adversary. State power is no more to be used so as to handicap religions than it is to favor them.

. . . The State contributes no money to the schools. It does not support them. Its legislation, as applied, does no more than provide a general program to help parents get their children, regardless of their religion, safely and expeditiously to and from accredited schools.

The First Amendment has erected a wall between church and state. That wall must be kept high and impregnable. We could not approve the slightest breach. New Jersey has not breached it here. Affirmed.

Illinois ex rel. McCollum v. Board of Education, 333 U.S. 203 (1948)

. . . Vashti McCollum [was] . . . a resident and taxpayer of Champaign and . . . a parent whose child was then enrolled in the Champaign public schools. Illinois has a compulsory education law which, with exceptions, requires parents to send their children, aged seven to sixteen, to its tax-supported public schools, where the children are to remain in attendance during the hours when the schools are regularly in session. Parents who violate this law commit a misdemeanor punishable by fine unless the children attend private or parochial schools which meet educational standards fixed by the State.

. . . In 1940, interested members of the Jewish, Roman Catholic, and a few of the Protestant faiths formed a voluntary association called the Champaign Council on Religious Education. They obtained permission from the Board of Education to offer classes in religious instruction to public school pupils in grades four to nine, inclusive. Classes were made up of pupils whose parents signed printed cards requesting that their children be permitted to attend; they were held weekly, thirty minutes for the lower grades, forty-five minutes for the higher. The council employed the religious teachers at no expense to the school authorities, but the instructors were subject to the approval and supervision of the superintendent of schools. The classes were taught in three separate religious groups by Protestant teachers, Catholic priests, and a Jewish rabbi. . . . Classes were conducted in the regular classrooms of the school building. Students who did not choose to take the religious instruction were not released from public school duties; they were required to leave their classrooms and go to some other place in the school building for pursuit of their secular studies. On the other hand, students who were released from secular study for the religious instructions were required to be present at the religious classes. Reports of their presence or absence were to be made to their secular teachers.

The foregoing facts . . . show the use of tax supported property for religious instruction and the close cooperation between the school authorities and the religious council in promoting religious education. The operation of the State's compulsory education system thus assists and is integrated with the program of religious instruction carried on by separate religious sects. Pupils compelled by law to go to school for secular education are released in part from their legal duty upon the condition that they attend the religious classes. This is beyond all question a utilization of the tax-established and tax-supported public school system to aid religious groups to spread their faith. And it falls squarely under the ban of the First Amendment (made applicable to the States by the Fourteenth) . . . counsel for the respondents challenge those views as dicta, and urge that we reconsider and repudiate them. They argue that, historically, the First Amendment was intended to forbid only government preference of one religion over another, not an impartial governmental assistance of all religions. In addition, they ask that we distinguish or overrule our holding in the Everson case that the Fourteenth Amendment made the "establishment of religion" clause of the First Amendment applicable as a prohibition against the States. After giving full consideration to the arguments presented, we are unable to accept either of these contentions.

To hold that a state cannot, consistently with the First and Fourteenth Amendments, utilize its public school system to aid any or all religious faiths or sects in the dissemination of their doctrines and ideals does not, as counsel urge, manifest a governmental hostility to religion or religious teachings. A manifestation of such hostility would be at war with our national tradition as embodied in the First Amendment's guaranty of the free exercise of religion. For the First Amendment rests upon the premise that both religion and government can best work to achieve their lofty aims if each is left free from the other within its respective sphere. Or, as we said in the Everson case, the First Amendment has erected a wall between Church and State which must be kept high and impregnable.

Here not only are the State's tax-supported public school buildings used for the dissemination of religious doctrines. The State also affords sectarian groups an invaluable aid in that it helps to provide pupils for their religious classes through use of the State's compulsory public school machinery. This is not separation of Church and State. The cause is reversed and remanded to the State Supreme Court for proceedings not inconsistent with this opinion. Reversed and remanded.

Zorach v. Clauson, 343 U.S. 306 (1952)

Mr. Justice Douglas delivered the opinion of the Court.

New York City has a program which permits its public schools to release students during the school day so that they may leave the school buildings and school grounds and go to religious centers for religious instruction or devotional exercises. A student is released on written request of his parents. Those not released stay in the classrooms. The churches make weekly reports to the schools, sending a list of children who have been released from public school but who have not reported for religious instruction.

This "released time" program involves neither religious instruction in public school classrooms nor the expenditure of public funds. All costs, including the application blanks, are paid by the religious organizations. The case is therefore unlike *McCollum v. Board of Education* . . . which involved a "released time" program from Illinois. In that case, the classrooms were turned over to religious instructors. We accordingly held that the program violated the First Amendment which (by reason of the Fourteenth Amendment) prohibits the states from establishing religion or prohibiting its free exercise.

Appellants, who are taxpayers and residents of New York City and whose children attend its public schools, challenge the present law, contending it is, in essence, not different from the one involved in the McCollum case. . . . It takes obtuse reasoning to inject any issue of the "free exercise" of religion into the present case. No one is forced to go to the religious classroom, and no religious exercise or instruction is brought to the classrooms of the public schools. . . . There is a suggestion that the system involves the use of coercion to get public school students into religious classrooms. There is no evidence in the record before us that supports that conclusion. . . . Moreover, apart from that claim of coercion, we do not see how New York by this type of "released time" program has made a law respecting an establishment of religion within the meaning of the First Amendment. . . . There cannot be the slightest doubt that the First Amendment reflects the philosophy that Church and State should be separated. . . . The First Amendment, however, does not say that, in every and all respects there shall be a separation of Church and State. Rather, it studiously defines the manner, the specific ways, in which there shall be no concert or union or dependency one on the other. That is the common sense of the matter. Otherwise the state and religion would be aliens to each other—hostile, suspicious, and even unfriendly. Churches could not be required to pay even property taxes. Municipalities would not be permitted to render police or fire protection to religious groups. . . . A fastidious atheist or agnostic could even object to the supplication with which the Court opens each session: "God save the United States and this Honorable Court."

We are a religious people whose institutions presuppose a Supreme Being. We guarantee the freedom to worship as one chooses. We make room for as wide a variety of beliefs and creeds as the spiritual needs of man deem necessary. We sponsor an attitude on the part of government that shows no partiality to any one group and that lets each flourish according to the zeal of its adherents and the appeal of its dogma. When the state encourages religious instruction or cooperates with religious authorities by adjusting the schedule of public events to sectarian needs, it follows the best of our traditions. For it then respects the religious nature of our people and accommodates the public service to their spiritual needs. To hold that it may not would be to find in the Constitution a requirement that the government show a callous indifference to religious groups. That would be preferring those who believe in no religion over those who do believe. Government may not finance religious groups nor undertake religious instruction nor blend secular and sectarian education nor use secular institutions to force one or some religion on any person. But we find no constitutional requirement which makes it necessary for government to be hostile to religion and to throw its weight against efforts to widen the effective scope of religious influence. The government must be neutral when it comes to competition between sects. It may not thrust any sect on any person. It may not make a religious observance compulsory. It may not coerce anyone to attend church, to observe a religious holiday, or to take religious instruction. But it can close its doors or suspend its operations as to those who want to repair to their religious sanctuary for worship or instruction. No more than that is undertaken here. Affirmed.

Engel v. Vitale, 370 U.S. 421 (1962)

Mr. Justice Black delivered the opinion of the Court.

The respondent Board of Education of Union Free School District No. 9, New Hyde Park, New York, acting in its official capacity under state law, directed the School District's principal to cause the following prayer to be said aloud by each class in the presence of a teacher at the beginning of each school day: Almighty God, we acknowledge our dependence upon Thee, and we beg Thy blessings upon us, our parents, our teachers and our Country.

This daily procedure was adopted on the recommendation of the State Board of Regents, a governmental agency. . . . [T]he parents of ten pupils brought this action in a New York State Court insisting that use of this official prayer in the public schools was contrary to the beliefs, religions, or religious practices of both themselves and their children . . . [and that the] regulation ordering the recitation of this particular prayer on the ground that these actions of official governmental agencies violate that part of the First Amendment of the Federal Constitution which commands that "Congress shall make no law respecting an establishment of religion." We think that, by using its public school system to encourage recitation of the Regents' prayer, the State of New York has adopted a practice wholly inconsistent with the Establishment Clause. There can, of course, be no doubt that New York's program of daily classroom invocation of God's blessings as prescribed in the Regents' prayer is a religious activity. It is a solemn avowal of divine faith and supplication for the blessings of the Almighty. The nature of such a prayer has always been religious, none of the respondents has denied this, and the trial court expressly so found . . .

There can be no doubt that New York's state prayer program officially establishes the religious beliefs embodied in the Regents' prayer. The respondents' argument to the contrary, which is largely based upon the contention that the Regents' prayer is "nondenominational" and the fact that the program, as modified and approved by state courts, does not require all pupils to recite the prayer, but permits those who wish to do so to remain silent or be excused from the room, ignores the essential nature of the program's constitutional defects. Neither the fact that the prayer may be denominationally neutral nor the fact that its observance on the part of the students is voluntary can serve to free it from the limitations of the Establishment Clause, as it might from the Free Exercise Clause, of the First Amendment, both of which are operative against the States by virtue of the Fourteenth Amendment. Although these two clauses may, in certain instances, overlap, they forbid two quite different kinds of governmental encroachment upon religious freedom. The Establishment Clause, unlike the Free Exercise Clause, does not depend upon any showing of direct governmental compulsion and is violated by the enactment of laws which establish an official religion whether those laws operate directly to coerce nonobserving individuals or not. This is not to say, of course, that laws officially prescribing a particular form of religious worship do not involve coercion of such individuals. When the power, prestige and financial support of government is placed behind a particular religious belief, the indirect coercive pressure upon religious minorities to conform to the prevailing officially approved religion is plain. But the purposes underlying the Establishment Clause go much further than that. Its first and most immediate purpose rested on the belief that a union of government and religion tends to destroy government and to degrade religion. . . . The New York laws officially prescribing the Regents' prayer are inconsistent both with the purposes of the Establishment Clause and with the Establishment Clause itself. Reversed and remanded.

School District of Abington Township, Pennsylvania v. Schempp, 374 U.S. 203 (1963)

[A Pennsylvania law required that] at least ten verses from the Holy Bible shall be read, without comment, at the opening of each public school on each school day. Any child shall be excused from such Bible reading, or attending such Bible reading, upon the written request of his parent or guardian.

The Schempp family, husband and wife and two of their three children, brought suit to enjoin enforcement of the statute, contending that their rights under the Fourteenth Amendment to the Constitution of the United States are, have been, and will continue to be, violated unless this statute be declared unconstitutional as violative of these provisions of the First Amendment. . . .

On each school day at the Abington Senior High School between 8:15 and 8:30 A.M., while the pupils are attending their home rooms or advisory sections, opening exercises are conducted pursuant to the statute. The exercises are broadcast into each room in the school building through an intercommunications system, and are conducted under the supervision of a teacher by students attending the school's radio and television workshop. Selected students from this course gather each morning in the school's workshop studio for the exercises, which include readings by one of the students of 10 verses of the Holy Bible, broadcast to each room in the building. This is followed by the recitation of the Lord's Prayer, likewise over the intercommunications system, but also by the students in the various classrooms, who are asked to stand and join in repeating the prayer in unison. The exercises are closed with the flag salute and such pertinent announcements as are of interest to the students. Participation in the opening exercises, as directed by the statute, is voluntary. The student reading the verses from the Bible may select the passages and read from any version he chooses, although the only copies furnished by the school are the King James version, copies of which were circulated to each teacher by the school district. During the period in which the exercises have been conducted, the King James, the Douay, and the Revised Standard versions of the Bible have been used, as well as the Jewish Holy Scriptures. There are no prefatory statements, no questions asked or solicited, no comments or explanations made, and no interpretations given at or during the exercises. The students and parents are advised that the student may absent himself from the classroom or, should he elect to remain, not participate in the exercises. . . .

The reading of the verses, even without comment, possesses a devotional and religious character and constitutes, in effect, a religious observance. The devotional and religious nature of the morning exercises is made all the more apparent by the fact that the Bible reading is followed immediately by a recital in unison by the pupils of the Lord's Prayer. The fact that some pupils, or, theoretically, all pupils, might be excused from attendance at the exercises does not mitigate the obligatory nature of the ceremony. . . .

The fundamental concept of liberty embodied in that [Fourteenth] Amendment embraces the liberties guaranteed by the First Amendment. The First Amendment declares that Congress shall make no law respecting an establishment of religion or prohibiting the free exercise thereof. The Fourteenth Amendment has rendered the legislatures of the states as incompetent as Congress to enact such laws. . . .

[T]his Court has rejected unequivocally the contention that the Establishment Clause forbids only governmental preference of one religion over another. Almost 20 years ago in *Everson*, the Court said that "neither a state nor the Federal Government can set up a church. Neither can pass laws which aid one religion, aid all religions, or prefer one religion over another."

Lemon v. Kurtzman, 403 U.S. 602 (1971)

Burger, C.J., delivered the opinion of the Court.

These two appeals raise questions as to Pennsylvania and Rhode Island statutes providing state aid to church-related elementary and secondary schools. Both statutes are challenged as violative of the Establishment and Free Exercise Clauses of the First Amendment and the Due Process Clause of the Fourteenth Amendment.

Pennsylvania has adopted a statutory program that provides financial support to nonpublic elementary and secondary schools by way of reimbursement for the cost of teachers' salaries, textbooks, and instructional materials in specified secular subjects. Rhode Island has adopted a statute under which the State pays directly to teachers in nonpublic elementary schools a supplement of 15 percent of their annual salary. Under each statute, state aid has been given to church-related educational institutions. We hold that both statutes are unconstitutional. . . .

In *Everson v. Board of Education*, 330 U.S. 1 (1947), this Court upheld a state statute that reimbursed the parents of parochial school children for bus transportation expenses. There, Mr. Justice Black, writing for the majority, suggested that the decision carried to "the verge" of forbidden territory under the Religion Clauses. Candor compels acknowledgment, moreover, that we can only dimly perceive the lines of demarcation in this extraordinarily sensitive area of constitutional law.

The language of the Religion Clauses of the First Amendment is, at best, opaque, particularly when compared with other portions of the Amendment. Its authors did not simply prohibit the establishment of a state church or a state religion, an area history shows they regarded as very important and fraught with great dangers. Instead, they commanded that there should be "no law respecting an establishment of religion." A law may be one "respecting" the forbidden objective while falling short of its total realization. A law "respecting" the proscribed result, that is, the establishment of religion, is not always easily identifiable as one violative of the Clause. A given law might not establish a state religion, but nevertheless be one "respecting" that end in the sense of being a step that could lead to such establishment, and hence offend the First Amendment.

In the absence of precisely stated constitutional prohibitions, we must draw lines with reference to the three main evils against which the Establishment Clause was intended to afford protection: "sponsorship, financial support, and active involvement of the sovereign in religious activity." *Walz v. Tax Commission*, 397 U.S. 664, 668 (1970). . . .

The two legislatures, however, have also recognized that church-related elementary and secondary schools have a significant religious mission, and that a substantial portion of their activities is religiously oriented. They have therefore sought to create statutory restrictions designed to guarantee the separation between secular and religious educational functions, and to ensure that State financial aid supports only the former. All these provisions are precautions taken in candid recognition that these programs approached, even if they did not intrude upon, the forbidden areas under the Religion Clauses. We need not decide whether these legislative precautions restrict the principal or primary effect of the programs to the point where they do not offend the Religion Clauses, for we conclude that the cumulative impact of the entire relationship arising under the statutes in each State involves excessive entanglement between government and religion. . . .

Our prior holdings do not call for total separation between church and state; total separation is not possible in an absolute sense. Some relationship between government and religious organizations is inevitable. . . .

[T]he District Court concluded that the parochial schools constituted "an integral part of the religious mission of the Catholic Church." The various characteristics of the schools make them "a powerful vehicle for transmitting the Catholic faith to the next generation." This process of inculcating religious doctrine is, of course, enhanced by the impressionable age of the pupils, in primary schools particularly. In short, parochial schools involve substantial religious activity and purpose.

The substantial religious character of these church-related schools gives rise to entangling church-state relationships of the kind the Religion Clauses sought to avoid. . . .

Several teachers testified, however, that they did not inject religion into their secular classes. And the District Court found that religious values did not necessarily affect the content of the secular instruction. But what has been recounted suggests the potential, if not actual, hazards of this form of state aid. The teacher is employed by a religious organization, subject to the direction and discipline of religious authorities, and works in a system dedicated to rearing children in a particular faith. These controls are not lessened by the fact that most of the lay teachers are of the Catholic faith. Inevitably, some of a teacher's responsibilities hover on the border between secular and religious orientation. . . .

Finally, nothing we have said can be construed to disparage the role of church-related elementary and secondary schools in our national life. Their contribution has been and is enormous. Nor do we ignore their economic plight in a period of rising costs and expanding need. Taxpayers generally have been spared vast sums by the maintenance of these educational institutions by religious organizations, largely by the gifts of faithful adherents.

The merit and benefits of these schools, however, are not the issue before us in these cases. The sole question is whether state aid to these schools can be squared with the dictates of the Religion Clauses. Under our system, the choice has been made that government is to be entirely excluded from the area of religious instruction, and churches excluded from the affairs of government. The Constitution decrees that religion must be a private matter for the individual, the family, and the institutions of private choice, and that, while some involvement and entanglement are inevitable, lines must be drawn.

Lee v. Weisman, 505 U.S. 577 (1992)

Justice Kennedy delivered the opinion of the Court.

School principals in the public school system of the city of Providence, Rhode Island, are permitted to invite members of the clergy to offer invocation and benediction prayers as part of the formal graduation ceremonies for middle schools and for high schools. The question before us is whether including clerical members who offer prayers as part of the official school graduation ceremony is consistent with the Religion Clauses of the First Amendment, provisions the Fourteenth Amendment makes applicable with full force to the States and their school districts.

Deborah Weisman graduated from Nathan Bishop Middle School, a public school in Providence, at a formal ceremony in June 1989. She was about 14 years old. For many years it has been the policy of the Providence School Committee and the Superintendent of Schools to permit principals to invite members of the clergy to give invocations and benedictions at middle school and high school graduations. Many, but not all, of the principals elected to include prayers as part of the graduation ceremonies. Acting for himself and his daughter, Deborah's father, Daniel Weisman, objected to any prayers at Deborah's middle school graduation, but to no avail. The school principal, petitioner Robert E. Lee, invited a rabbi to deliver prayers at the graduation exercises for Deborah's class. Rabbi Leslie Gutterman, of the Temple Beth El in Providence, accepted.

It has been the custom of Providence school officials to provide invited clergy with a pamphlet entitled "Guidelines for Civic Occasions," prepared by the National Conference of Christians and Jews. The Guidelines recommend that public prayers at nonsectarian civic ceremonies be composed with "inclusiveness and sensitivity," though they acknowledge that "prayer of any kind may be inappropriate on some civic occasions." The principal gave Rabbi Gutterman the pamphlet before the graduation and advised him the invocation and benediction should be nonsectarian.

Rabbi Gutterman's prayers were as follows:

Invocation:
God of the Free, Hope of the Brave:
For the legacy of America where diversity is celebrated
    and the rights of minorities are protected, we thank
    You. May these young men and women grow up to
    enrich it.
For the liberty of America, we thank You. May these
    new graduates grow up to guard it.
For the political process of America in which all its citi-
    zens may participate, for its court system where all
    may seek justice we thank You. May those we
    honor this morning always turn to it in trust.
For the destiny of America we thank You. May the grad-
    uates of Nathan Bishop Middle School so live that
    they might help to share it.
May our aspirations for our country and for these
    young people, who are our hope for the future, be
    richly fulfilled.
Amen.

Benediction:
O God, we are grateful to You for having endowed us
    with the capacity for learning which we have cele-
    brated on this joyous commencement.

Happy families give thanks for seeing their children
achieve an important milestone. Send Your blessings upon the teachers and administrators who
helped prepare them.
The graduates now need strength and guidance for the
future, help them to understand that we are not
complete with academic knowledge alone. We
must each strive to fulfill what You require of us all:
To do justly, to love mercy, to walk humbly.
We give thanks to You, Lord, for keeping us alive, sus-
taining us and allowing us to reach this special,
happy occasion.
Amen.

. . . Deborah [Weisman] and her family attended the graduation, where the prayers were recited. In July 1989, Daniel Weisman [her father] filed an amended complaint seeking a
permanent injunction barring petitioners, various officials of the
Providence public schools, from inviting the clergy to deliver
invocations and benedictions at future graduations. . . . The District Court [granted an injuction] . . . based on its reading of our
precedents. . . . The court determined that the practice of including invocations and benedictions, even so-called nonsectarian
ones, in public school graduations creates an identification of
governmental power with religious practice, endorses religion,
and violates the Establishment Clause. . . . On appeal, the
United States Court of Appeals for the First Circuit affirmed. . . .
We granted certiorari, and now affirm.

The principle that government may accommodate the free
exercise of religion does not supersede the fundamental limitations imposed by the Establishment Clause. It is beyond dispute
that, at a minimum, the Constitution guarantees that government may not coerce anyone to support or participate in religion or its exercise, or otherwise act in a way which "establishes
a [state] religion or religious faith, or tends to do so." The
State's involvement in the school prayers challenged today violates these central principles. . . .

Divisiveness, of course, can attend any state decision respecting religions, and neither its existence nor its potential necessarily invalidates the State's attempts to accommodate
religion in all cases. The potential for divisiveness is of particular relevance here though, because it centers around an overt religious exercise in a secondary school environment where, as

we discuss below, subtle coercive pressures exist and where the student had no real alternative which would have allowed her to avoid the fact or appearance of participation. . . .

The degree of school involvement here made it clear that the graduation prayers bore the imprint of the State and thus put school-age children who objected in an untenable position. We turn our attention now to consider the position of the students, both those who desired the prayer and she who did not. . . .

We need not look beyond the circumstances of this case to see the phenomenon at work. The undeniable fact is that the school district's supervision and control of a high school graduation ceremony places public pressure, as well as peer pressure, on attending students to stand as a group or, at least, maintain respectful silence during the Invocation and Benediction. This pressure, though subtle and indirect, can be as real as any overt compulsion. Of course, in our culture standing or remaining silent can signify adherence to a view or simple respect for the views of others. And no doubt some persons who have no desire to join a prayer have little objection to standing as a sign of respect for those who do. But for the dissenter of high school age, who has a reasonable perception that she is being forced by the State to pray in a manner her conscience will not allow, the injury is no less real. There can be no doubt that for many, if not most, of the students at the graduation, the act of standing or remaining silent was an expression of participation in the Rabbi's prayer. That was the very point of the religious exercise. It is of little comfort to a dissenter, then, to be told that for her the act of standing or remaining in silence signifies mere respect, rather than participation. What matters is that, given our social conventions, a reasonable dissenter in this milieu could believe that the group exercise signified her own participation or approval of it. . . .

We do not hold that every state action implicating religion is invalid if one or a few citizens find it offensive. People may take offense at all manner of religious as well as nonreligious messages, but offense alone does not in every case show a violation. We know too that sometimes to endure social isolation or even anger may be the price of conscience or nonconformity. But, by any reading of our cases, the conformity required of the student in this case was too high an exaction to withstand the test of the Establishment Clause. The prayer exercises in this case are especially improper because the State has in every practical sense compelled attendance and participation in an explicit religious exercise at an event of singular importance to every student, one the objecting student had no real alternative to avoid. . . .

Affirmed.

Agostini v. Felton (1997)

Justice O'Connor delivered the opinion of the Court.

In 1965, Congress enacted Title I of the Elementary and Secondary Education Act of 1965, . . . to "provid[e] full educational opportunity to every child regardless of economic background.". . .

Petitioner Board of Education of the City of New York (Board), an LEA, first applied for Title I funds in 1966 and has grappled ever since with how to provide Title I services to the private school students within its jurisdiction. Approximately 10 percent of the total number of students eligible for Title I services are private school students. . . . [T]he Board initially arranged to transport children to public schools for after school Title I instruction. But this enterprise was largely unsuccessful. Attendance was poor, teachers and children were tired, and parents were concerned for the safety of their children. The Board then moved the after school instruction onto private school campuses. . . .

That plan called for the provision of Title I services on private school premises during school hours. Under the plan, only public employees could serve as Title I instructors and counselors. . . . [A] large majority of Title I teachers worked in nonpublic schools with religious affiliations different from their own. The vast majority of Title I teachers also moved among the private schools, spending fewer than five days a week at the same school. . . .

In 1978, six federal taxpayers . . . sued the Board in the District Court for the Eastern District of New York. Respondents sought declaratory and injunctive relief, claiming that the Board's Title I program violated the Establishment Clause. . . . The District Court granted summary judgment for the Board, but the Court of Appeals for the Second Circuit reversed. . . . In a 5–4 decision, this Court [the U.S. Supreme Court] affirmed on the ground that the Board's Title I program necessitated an "excessive entanglement of church and state in the administration of [Title I] benefits.". . .

Rather than offer Title I instruction to parochial school students at their schools, the Board reverted to its prior practice of providing instruction at public school sites, at leased sites, and in mobile instructional units (essentially vans converted into classrooms) parked near the sectarian school. The Board also offered computer aided instruction, which could be provided "on premises" because it did not require public employees to be physically present on the premises of a religious school. . . .

In October and December of 1995, petitioners—the Board and a new group of parents of parochial school students entitled to Title I services—filed motions . . . calling for the overruling of Aguilar. The District Court denied the motion. . . . We granted certiorari . . . and now reverse. . . .

In order to evaluate whether Aguilar has been eroded by our subsequent Establishment Clause cases, it is necessary to understand the rationale upon which Aguilar . . . rested. . . .

Distilled to essentials, the Court's conclusion that the Shared Time program[s] . . . had the impermissible effect of advancing religion rested on three assumptions: (i) any public employee who works on the premises of a religious school is presumed to inculcate religion in her work; (ii) the presence of public employees on private school premises creates a symbolic union between church and state; and (iii) any and all public aid that directly aids the educational function of religious schools impermissibly finances religious indoctrination, even if the aid reaches such schools as a consequence of private decisionmaking. Additionally, in Aguilar there was a fourth assumption: that New York City's Title I program necessitated an excessive government entanglement with religion because public employees who teach on the premises of religious schools must be closely monitored to ensure that they do not inculcate religion.

Our more recent cases have undermined the assumptions upon which Ball and Aguilar relied. . . . Our cases subsequent to Aguilar have, however, modified in two significant respects the approach we use to assess indoctrination. First, we have abandoned the presumption erected . . . that the placement of public employees on parochial school grounds inevitably results in the impermissible effect of state sponsored indoctrination or constitutes a symbolic union between government and religion. In *Zobrest v. Catalina Foothills School District* (1993), we examined whether the IDEA was constitutional as applied to a deaf student who sought to bring his state employed sign language interpreter with him to his Roman Catholic high school. We held that this was permissible, expressly disavowing the notion that "the Establishment Clause [laid] down [an] absolute bar to the placing of a public employee in a sectarian school." "Such a flat rule, smacking of antiquated notions of 'taint,' would indeed exalt form over substance.". . . Because the only government aid in *Zobrest* was the interpreter, who was herself not inculcating any religious messages, no government indoctrination took place and we were able to conclude that "the provision of such assistance [was] not barred by the Establishment Clause." *Zobrest* therefore expressly rejected the notion—relied on in Ball and Aguilar—that, solely because of her presence on private school property, a public employee will be presumed to inculcate religion in the students. *Zobrest* also implicitly repudiated another assumption on which Ball and Aguilar turned: that the presence of a public employee on private school property creates an impermissible "symbolic link" between government and religion. . . .

[T]here is no reason to presume that, simply because she enters a parochial school classroom, a full time public employee such as a Title I teacher will depart from her assigned duties and instructions and embark on religious indoctrination, any more than there was a reason in *Zobrest* to think an interpreter would inculcate religion by altering her translation of classroom lectures. . . . Nor under current law can we conclude that a program placing full time public employees on parochial campuses to provide Title I instruction would impermissibly finance religious indoctrination. . . . [T]urn[ing] . . . to Aguilar's conclusion that New York City's Title I program resulted in an excessive entanglement between church and state . . . [s]ince we have abandoned the assumption that properly instructed public employees will fail to discharge their duties faithfully, we must also discard the assumption that pervasive monitoring of Title I teachers is required [and does not] create an excessive entanglement.

We therefore hold that a federally funded program providing supplemental, remedial instruction to disadvantaged children on a neutral basis is not invalid under the Establishment Clause when such instructions given on the premises of sectarian schools by government employees pursuant to a program containing safeguards such as those present here. The same considerations that justify this holding require us to conclude that this carefully constrained program also cannot reasonably be viewed as an endorsement of religion. . . . Accordingly, we must acknowledge that *Aguilar* [is] no longer good law. . . . For these reasons, we reverse.

Quotations

Much has been written and spoken on the subject of religion in the public schools. Because the public schools are government-supported, the ultimate issue involves the separation of church and state. Even before the U.S. Constitution was written there had been controversy over church-state relations. Those, including James Madison, who wanted a strict wall of separation are referred to as "separationists." Others, like Patrick Henry, who wanted close cooperation and support between the government and churches are referred to as "accommodationists." These divisions continue today as many individuals argue for strict separation while others want to adopt a more cooperative approach. The following historical and contemporary quotations reflect the opinions of individuals on both sides of the issue.

Bill of Rights

The very purpose of a Bill of Rights was to withdraw certain subjects from the vicissitudes of political controversy, to place them beyond reach of majorities and officials and to establish them as legal principles to be applied by the courts. One's right to . . . freedom of worship and other fundamental rights may not be submitted to vote: they depend on the outcome of no elections.

> U.S. Supreme Court Justice Robert
> Jackson's majority opinion in *West Vir-*
> *ginia State Board of Education v. Barnette,*
> 319 U.S. 624 (1943)

Busing for Parochial School Students

It is undoubtedly true that children are helped to get to church schools [by the state's payment of their bus fares]. . . . Moreover, state-paid policemen, detailed to protect children going to and from church schools from the very real hazards of traffic, would serve much the same purpose and accomplish much the same results as state provisions intended to guarantee free transportation. . . . Of course cutting off church schools from these services . . . would make it far more difficult for the schools to operate. But such is obviously not the purpose of the First Amendment. That Amendment requires the state to be a neutral in its relations with groups of religious believers and non-believers; it does not require the state to be their adversary. State power is no more to be used so as to handicap religions than it is to favor them. . . . The State contributes no money to these [church] schools. It does not support them. Its legislation, as applied, does no more than provide a general program to help parents get their children, regardless of their religion, safely and expeditiously to and from accredited schools.

> U.S. Supreme Court Justice Hugo
> Black's majority opinion in *Everson v.*
> *Board of Education of the Township of*
> *Ewing, 330 U.S. 1* (1947), upholding
> New Jersey's free bus service for
> parochial school students

Censorship of Books Used in Schools

Like the thief who cries "Stop, thief" in order to distract attention from his own crime, many powerful liberals cry "censorship" in order to hide the fact that they are the most notorious censors of all.

> Phyllis Schlafly, *Fact and Fiction about*
> *Censorship* (1984)

Christian Schools

One day, I hope in the next ten years, I can trust that we will have more Christian day schools than there are public schools. I hope I live to see the day when, as in the early days of our country, we won't have any public schools. The churches will have taken over again and Christians will be running them. What a happy day that will be.

> Reverend Jerry Falwell, *America Can*
> *Be Saved* (1979)

Creationism

Evolutionism is the philosophy that purports to explain the origins and development of all things in terms of continuing natural processes in a self-existing universe. Creationism, on the other hand, explains the origin and development of all things by completed supernatural processes in a universe created and sustained by a transcendent, self-existing Creator.

Henry Morris, *Education for the Real World* (1978)

This question of creation or evolution is not merely a peripheral scientific issue, but rather is nothing less than the age-long conflict between God and Satan. . . . Any educational system for the training of the coming generation must and will seek to inculcate one or the other.

Henry Morris, *Education for the Real World* (1978)

Neither evolution nor creation is accessible to the scientific method, since they deal with origins and history, not with presently observable and repeatable events.

Henry Morris, "Evolution, Creation and the Public Schools" (1974)

What right have the evolutionists—a relatively small percentage of the population—to teach at public expense a so called scientific interpretation of the Bible, when Orthodox Christians are not permitted to teach an orthodox interpretation of the Bible.

William Jennings Bryan at Scopes trial (1925)

Diversity of Religious Practice

Those who begin coercive elimination of dissent soon find themselves exterminating dissenters. Compulsory unanimity of opinion achieves only the unanimity of the graveyard. . . . The First Amendment . . . was designed to avoid these endings by avoiding these beginnings. . . . No official, high or petty, can prescribe what shall be orthodox in politics, nationalism, religion, or other matters of opinion or force citizens to confess by word or act, their faith therein.

U.S. Supreme Court Justice Robert Jackson striking down a mandatory flag salute, *West Virginia State Board of Education v. Barnette*, 319 U.S. 624 (1943)

Establishment Clause

Who does not see that the same authority which can establish Christianity, in exclusion of all other Religions, may establish with the same ease, any particular sect of Christians, in exclusion of all other Sects?

> James Madison, quoted in Saul K.
> Padover, *The Complete Madison* (New
> York: Harper and Brothers, 1953), p. 301

In a community where such a large number of pupils are served by church-related schools, it can be assumed that state assistance will entail considerable political activity. Partisans of parochial schools . . . will inevitably champion this cause and promote political action to achieve their goal. Those who oppose state aid [to parochial schools] will inevitably respond and employ all of the usual political campaign techniques to prevail. Candidates will be forced to declare and voters to choose.

Ordinary political debate and division, however vigorous or even partisan, are normal and healthy manifestations of our democratic system of government, but political division along religious lines was one of the principal evils against which the First Amendment was intended to protect. . . . To have States or communities divide on the issues presented by state aid to parochial schools would tend to confuse and obscure other issues of great urgency. . . . It conflicts with our whole history and tradition to permit questions of the Religion Clauses to assume such an importance in our legislatures and in our elections.

> U.S. Supreme Court Justice William
> Brennan's concurring opinion in *Meek
> v. Pettinger* (1975)

The phrase "establishment of religion" must be given the meaning that it had in the United States in 1791, rather than its European connotation. In America there was no establishment of a single church, as in England. Four states had never adopted any establishment practices. Three had abolished their establishments during the Revolution. The remaining six states . . . changed to comprehensive or "multiple" establishments. That is, aid was provided to all churches. . . . It was this nonpreferential

assistance to organized churches that constituted "establishment of religion" in 1791, and it was this practice that the [First]
Amendment forbade Congress to adopt.

> C. Herman Pritchett, *The American
> Constitution,* 3d ed. (New York:
> McGraw-Hill: 1977)

Had the framers prohibited"*the* establishment of religion"
which would have emphasized the generic word "religion,"
there might have been some reasoning for thinking they wanted
to prohibit all official preferences of religion over irreligion. But
by choosing "an establishment" over "the establishment," they
were showing that they wanted to prohibit only those official
activities that tended to promote the interests of one or another
particular sect. . . . The Northwest ordinance of 1787 . . . set
aside some of the federal lands in the territory for schools . . .
[which] were expected to promote religion as well as morality.
In fact, most schools at this time were church-run sectarian
schools.

> Michael J. Malbin, *Religion and Politics*
> (1977)

It is clear to me that past practice shows such cooperation
[between churches and public schools] is not forbidden by the
First Amendment. When actual church services have always
been permitted on government property, the mere use of the
school buildings by a non-sectarian group for religious purposes ought not to be condemned as an establishment of
religion.

> U.S. Supreme Court Justice Reed's dis-
> senting opinion that disallowed release
> time for religious instruction in public
> school buildings in *McCollum v. Board
> of Education* (1948)

The Establishment Clause, unlike the Free Exercise Clause,
does not depend upon any showing of direct governmental
compulsion and is violated by the enactment of laws which establish an official religion whether those laws operate directly to
coerce nonobserving individuals or not. . . . When the power,

prestige and financial support of government is placed behind a particular religious belief, the indirect coercive pressure upon religious minorities to conform to the prevailing officially approved religion is plain.

Congress should not establish a religion and enforce the legal observation of it by law, nor compel men to worship God in any manner contrary to their conscience, or that one sect might obtain a pre-eminence, or two combined together, and establish a religion to which they would compel others to conform.

James Madison, *Annals of Congress,*
Saturday, August 15, 1789.

Evolution

Arkansas' law [prohibiting the teaching of evolution] cannot be defended as an act of religious neutrality. Arkansas did not seek to excise from the curricula of its schools and universities all discussion of the origin of man. The law's efforts were confined to an attempt to blot out a particular theory [evolution] because of its supposed conflict with the biblical account, literally read. Plainly, the law is contrary to the mandate of the First, and in violation of the Fourteenth Amendment to the Constitution.

U.S. Supreme Court Justice Abe Fortas'
majority opinion in *Epperson v.
Arkansas* (1968)

Government Protection of Religious Practice

As to religion, I hold it to be the indispensable duty of government to protect all conscientious professions thereof, and I know of no other business which government hath to do therewith.

Thomas Paine, *Common Sense* (1776)

Graduation Invocations

The mixing of government and religion can be a threat to free government, even if no one is forced to participate.

U.S. Supreme Court Justice Sandra Day
O'Connor's concurring opinion in *Lee
v. Weisman* (1992)

In holding that the Establishment Clause prohibits invocations and benedictions at public-school graduation ceremonies, the Court . . . lays waste a tradition that is as old as public-school graduation ceremonies themselves. . . . As its instrument of destruction, the bulldozer of its social engineering, the Court invents a boundless and boundlessly manipulable, test of psychological coercion.

The Court presumably would separate graduation invocations and benedictions from the other instances of public "preservation and transmission of religious beliefs" on the ground that they involve "psychological coercion." I find it a sufficient embarrassment that our Establishment Clause jurisprudence regarding holiday displays . . . has come to require scrutiny more commonly associated with interior decorators than with the judiciary. . . . But interior decorating is hard-rock science compared to psychology practiced by amateurs. . . . The Court's argument that state officials have "coerced" students to take part in the invocation and benediction at graduation ceremonies is, not to put too fine a point on it, incoherent.

U.S. Supreme Court Justice Antonin
Scalia's dissenting opinion in *Lee v.
Weisman* (1992)

Nondenominational Prayers

The Court today says that the state and federal governments are without constitutional power to prescribe any particular form of words to be recited by any group of the American people on any subject touching religion. The third stanza of "The Star-Spangled Banner," made our National Anthem by Act of Congress in 1931, contains these verses:

> Blest with victory and peace, may the heav'n rescued land
> Praise the Pow'r that hath made and preserved us a nation!
> Then conquer we must, when our cause it is just,
> And this be our motto In God is our Trust.

I do not believe that this Court, or the Congress, or the President by the actions and practices I have mentioned established an "official religion" in violation of the Constitution.

U.S. Supreme Court Justice Potter
Stewart's dissenting opinion in the

school prayer case, invalidating New
York state's nondenominational school
prayer, *Engel v. Vitale* (1962)

Original Intent of the Founders

A too literal quest for the advice of the Founding Fathers upon
the issues of these cases [Bible reading and recitation of the
Lord's Prayer in class] seems to me futile and misdirected for
several reasons. First, . . . the historical record is at best ambiguous, and statements can readily be found to support either
side of the proposition. . . . While it is clear to me that the
Framers [of the Constitution] meant the Establishment Clause
to prohibit more than the creation of established churches, they
gave no distinct consideration to the particular question
whether the clause also forbade devotional exercises in public
institutions.

U.S. Supreme Court Justice William
Brennan's concurring opinion in *Abington School District v. Schempp* (1963)

Pledge of Allegiance
(as Compulsory in School)

The religious liberty which the Constitution protects has never
excluded legislation of general scope not directed against doc-
trinal loyalties or particular sects. . . . The mere possession of religious convictions which contradict the relevant concerns of a
political society does not relieve the citizen from the discharge
of political responsibility.

U.S. Supreme Court Justice Felix Frankfurter's majority opinion in which the
Supreme Court denied the right of schoolchildren to refrain from reciting the pledge
of allegiance on religious grounds, *Minersville School District v. Gobitis* (1940)

Words uttered under coercion are proof of loyalty to nothing but self-interest. Love of country must spring from willing
hearts and free minds, inspired by a fair administration of wise

laws enacted by the people's elected representatives within the bounds of express constitutional prohibitions.

> U.S. Supreme Court Justice Robert Jackson's majority opinion in which the Supreme Court upheld the right of schoolchildren to refrain from reciting the pledge of allegiance on religious grounds, *Board of Education v. Barnette* (1943)

Prayer (in General)

I have lived, Sir, a long time, and the longer I live, the more convincing proofs I see of this truth—that God Governs in the affairs of men. And if an arrow cannot fall to the ground without his notice, is it probable that an empire can rise without his aid? . . . I therefore beg leave to move—that henceforth prayers imploring the assistance of Heaven, and its blessings on our deliberations, be held in this Assembly every morning before we proceed robustness, and that one or more of the Clergy of this City be requested to officiate in that Service.

> George Washington, addressing the Constitutional Convention (1787)

Public Funds

No tax in any amount, large or small, can be levied to support any religious activities or institutions, whatever they may be called, or whatever form they adopt to teach or practice religion. Neither a state nor the Federal Government can, openly or secretly, participate in the affairs of any religious organizations or groups or vice versa.

> U.S. Supreme Court Justice Hugo Black's unanimous majority opinion in *Everson v. Board of Education* (1947)

Purpose of Public Schools

The assimilation and education of our foreign born citizens in the principles of our government, the hopes and inspirations of our people, are best secured by and through attendance of all

children in our public schools. . . . Our children must not under
any pretext, be it based on money, creed, or social status, be divided into antagonistic groups, there to absorb the narrow
views of life as they are taught.

> Oregon Voter's Pamphlet, explaining an
> initiative proposal to ban all private and
> parochial schools and require attendance
> at public schools. The measure was ap-
> proved and enacted but declared uncon-
> stitutional by the U.S. Supreme Court in
> *Pierce v. Society of Sisters* (1925)

Release Time

We are a religious people whose institutions presuppose a
Supreme Being. We guarantee the freedom to worship as one
chooses. We make room for as wide a variety of beliefs and
creeds as the spiritual needs of man deem necessary. We sponsor
an attitude on the part of government that shows no partiality to
any one group and that lets each flourish according to the zeal of
its adherents and the appeal of its dogma. When the state encourages religious instruction or cooperates with religious instruction
by adjusting [school] schedules . . . it follows the best of our traditions. For it then respects the religious nature of our people and
accommodates the public service to their spiritual needs.

> U.S. Supreme Court Justice William O.
> Douglas's majority opinion upholding
> New York's release time program in
> *Zorach v. Clausen* (1952)

[In release time] formalized religious instructions substituted for other school activity. . . . The school system is very
much in operation during this kind of released time.

> U.S. Supreme Court Justice Felix
> Frankfurter's dissenting opinion in
> *Zorach v. Clausen* (1952)

The greater effectiveness of this system over voluntary attendance after school hours is due to the truant officer who, if
the youngster fails to go to school, dogs him back to the public

schoolroom. [The schoolroom] serves as a temporary jail for a pupil who will not go to Church. It takes more subtlety of mind than I possess to deny that this is governmental constraint in support of religion.

> U.S. Supreme Court Justice Robert H. Jackson's dissenting opinion in *Zorach v. Clausen* (1952)

Religion at Public Universities

I am not surprised at the dilemma produced at your University by making theological professorships an integral part of the system. The anticipation of such a one led to the omission in ours; the visitors being merely authorized to open a public hall for religious occasions, under impartial regulations; with the opportunity to the different sects to establish theological schools so near that the students of the University may respectively attend the religious exercises in them. The village of Charlottesville, also, where different religious worships will be held, is also so near, that resort may conveniently be had to them.

A University with sectarian professorships becomes, of course, a sectarian monopoly: with professorships of rival sects, it would be an arena of Theological Gladiators. Without any such professorships, it may incur, for a time at least, the imputation of irreligious tendencies, if not designs. The last difficulty was thought more manageable than either of the others. On this view of the subject, there seems to be no alternative but between a public University without a theological professorship, and sectarian seminaries without a University.

> James Madison, letter to Edward Everett, Montpelier, Vermont, 18 March 1823

School Prayer

Not only is this prayer not a violation of the First Amendment . . . but a holding that it is such a violation would be in defiance of all American history, and such a holding would destroy a part of the essential foundation of the American governmental structure.

> Opinion of the New York Court of Appeals in *Engel v. Vitale,* which was overruled by the U.S. Supreme Court

We start down a rough road, when we begin to mix compulsory public education with compulsory godliness.

U.S. Supreme Court Justice Robert
Jackson invalidating Illinois' release
time program in *McCollum v. Board of
Education*, 333 U.S. 203 (1948)

[The founding fathers] knew that the First Amendment, which tried to put an end to governmental control of religion and of prayer, was not written to destroy either.

U.S. Supreme Court Justice Hugo
Black writing for the majority in
Engel v. Vitale (1962)

Almighty God, we acknowledge our dependence upon Thee, and we beg Thy blessings upon us, our parents, our teachers, and our country.

New York state Regent's nondenominational prayer struck down by the U.S.
Supreme Court in *Engel v. Vitale* (1962)

To deny the wish of these school children to join in reciting this prayer is to deny them the opportunity of sharing in the spiritual heritage of our Nation.

Supporters of prayer in school seek to restore traditional values. They call for a constitutional amendment to reaffirm and reestablish the original intent of the religious freedom clause of the First Amendment, that which has been stolen, twisted, and used against them. The issue, they insist, is the guaranteed preservation of religious liberty.

Russ Walton, *Biblical Solutions to Contemporary Problems: A Handbook* (1988)

When the U.S. Supreme Court prohibited children from participating in voluntary prayers in public schools, the conclusion is inescapable that the Supreme Court not only violated the right of free exercise of religion for all Americans, it also established a national religion in the United States—the religion of secular humanism.

U.S. Senator Jesse Helms's Introduction to

Homer Duncan's *Secular Humanism, the
Most Dangerous Religion in America* (1979),
Lubbock, TX, Missionary Crusaders

There is nothing in any U.S. Supreme Court ruling to stop a
pupil from saying a prayer, either spoken or silent, at any time
the spirit moves him or her to do so, provided only that normal
school activity is not disrupted.

Samuel Rabinove, "Religious Liberty
and Church State Separation," *Vital
Speeches of the Day* (1986), p. 527

Secular and Sectarian

It is idle to pretend that this task is one for which we can find in
the Constitution one word to help us as judges to decide where
the secular ends and the sectarian begins in education. Nor can
we find guidance in any other legal source. It is a matter on
which we can find no law but our own prepossessions.

U.S. Supreme Court Justice Robert
Jackson's concurring opinion in *McCollum v. Board of Education* (1948)

Secular Humanism

Inasmuch as humanistic curriculum programs and "values-clar-
ification" and "moral-education" teaching strategies are based
upon materialistic values found only in man's nature itself, they
reject the spiritual and moral radiation of theistic faith and religion. Thus many parents who subscribe to Judaeo-Christian belief oppose humanistic education in the tax-supported schools
on grounds that such programs promote and advocate the religion of secular humanism in violation of the First Amendment
to the U.S. Constitution.

Onalee McGraw, *Secular Humanism and
the Schools: The Issue Whose Time Has
Come* (1976)

Today, public education is so humanistic that it is both anti-
Catholic and anti-Protestant—because it's anti-God. With the
expulsion of God from the schools, the view that man was cre-

ated by God and thus responsible for obeying His moral absolutes, deteriorated drastically. . . . [T]he chaos of today's public education system is in direct proportion to its religious obsession with humanism.

> Tim LaHaye, *The Battle for the Mind*
> (1980)

Control of children and education is control of the future. Humanists have always understood this. . . . Their purpose in promoting state control of education was twofold. First, they rightfully understood that the only way to destroy Biblical faith was to control the schools and, little by little, remove Christianity and introduce Humanism. Second, they were Centralists or statist, men who believed that salvation comes by work of statist legislation or laws.

> Rousas J. Rushdoony, *Intellectual Schizophrenia: Culture, Crisis and Education* (1973)

Separation of Church and State

Render therefore unto Caesar the things which are Caesar's and unto God the things that are God's.

> Matthew 22:21

As to religion, I hold it to be the indispensable duty of government to protect all conscientious professions thereof, and I know of no other business which government hath to do therewith.

> Thomas Paine, *Common Sense* (1776)

Separation means separation, not something else.

> U.S. Supreme Court Justice Felix Frankfurter's concurring opinion in *McCollum v. Board of Education* (1948)

The [First] Amendment's purpose was not to strike merely at the official establishment of a single sect, creed or religion, outlawing only a formal relation such as had prevailed in England and some of the colonies. . . . [T]he object was broader than separating church and state in this narrow sense. It was to create a complete and permanent separation of spheres of religious activity and civil authority by comprehensively forbidding every form of public aid or support for religion.

U.S. Supreme Court Justice Wiley Rutledge's dissenting opinion in *Everson v. Board of Education* (1947)

The civil Government, though bereft of everything like an associated hierarchy, possesses the requisite stability, and performs its functions with complete success, whilst the number, the industry, and the morality of the priesthood, and the devotion of the people, have been manifestly increased by the total separation of the church from the State.

James Madison, letter to Robert Walsh, 2 March 1819

Every new and successful example, therefore, of a perfect separation between the ecclesiastical and civil matters, is of importance; and I have no doubt that every new example will succeed, as every past one has done, in showing that religion and Government will both exist in greater purity the less they are mixed together.

James Madison, letter to Edward Livingston, 10 July 1822

The "wall of separation between Church and State" that Mr. Jefferson built at the University which he founded did not exclude religious education from the school. The difference between the generality of his statements on the separation of Church and State and the specificity of his conclusions on education are considerable. A rule of law should not be drawn from a figure of speech.

U.S. Supreme Court Justice Stanley Reed's dissenting opinion in *McCollum v. Board of Education* (1948) that disallowed release time religious instruction in public school buildings

There is much talk of the separation of Church and State in the history of the Bill of Rights and in the decisions clustering

around the First Amendment. . . . There cannot be the slightest
doubt that the First Amendment reflects the philosophy that the
Church and State should be separated. And so far as interference with the "free exercise" of religion and "establishment" of
religion are concerned, the separation must be complete and
unequivocal. The First Amendment within the scope of its coverage permits no exception; the prohibition is absolute. The
First Amendment, however, does not say that in every and all
respects there shall be a separation of Church and State. Rather,
it studiously defines the manner, the specific ways, in which
there shall be no concert or union or dependency on the other.
That is the common sense of the matter. Otherwise, the state
and religion would be aliens to each other—hostile, suspicious,
and even unfriendly. Churches could not be required to pay
even property taxes. Municipalities would not be permitted to
render police or fire protection to religious groups. . . . We
would have to press the concept of separation of church and
state to these extremes to condemn the present law on constitutional grounds.

> U.S. Supreme Court Justice William O.
> Douglas's majority opinion in *Zorach v.
> Clausen* (1952)

The Court thus creates an insoluble paradox for the State
and the parochial schools. The State cannot finance secular instruction if it permits religion to be taught in the same classroom; but if it exacts a promise that religion not be so taught—a
promise the schools and its teachers are quite willing and on
this record above to give—and enforces it, it is then entangled
in the "no entanglement" aspect of the Court's Establishment
Clause jurisprudence.

> U.S. Supreme Court Justice Byron
> White's lone dissent in *Lemon v. Kurtz-
> man* (1971).

State Support of Church-Affiliated University Facilities

But even he [James Madison] thought, as I do, that even a small
amount coming out of the pocket of taxpayers and going into

the coffers of a church was not in keeping with our constitutional ideal.

> U.S. Supreme Court Justice William O.
> Douglas's dissent in *Tilton v. Richardson*
> (1971)

State Support of Church-Established Schools

Because the bill vests in the said incorporated church an authority to provide for the support of the poor and the education of poor children of the same, an authority which, being altogether superfluous if the provision is to be the result of pious charity, would be a precedent for giving to religious societies as such a legal agency in carrying into effect a public and civil duty.

> James Madison, arguing against state
> support of schools and charitable activi-
> ties by churches, in the Congressional
> Record of 17 August 1789

Textbooks

When a student reads in a math book that there are no absolutes, every value he's been taught is destroyed. And the next thing you know, the students turn to crime and drugs. . . . Crime, violence, immorality and illiteracy . . . the seeds of decadence are being taught universally in schools.

> Mel and Norma Gabler, *Texas Monthly*
> (November 1982)

One may scan the acts in vain to ascertain where any money is appropriated for the purchase of school books for the use of any church, private, sectarian or even public school. The appropriations are made for the specific purpose of purchasing school books for the use of the school children of the state, free of cost to them. It was for their benefit and the resulting benefit to the state that the appropriations were made. . . . The schools, however, are not the beneficiaries of these appropriations. They obtain nothing from them, nor are they relieved of a single obligation because of them. The school children and the state are the beneficiaries.

Louisiana Supreme Court Justice
Charles Evans Hughes's majority opinion allowing public funds to be spent
for parochial school students in
Cochran v. Louisiana (1930). This logic
was later adopted by the U.S. Supreme
Court.

To bring charges against textbooks may sound extreme, but
we should be concerned. The vast majority of Americans are the
"Moral Majority." They want America to remain a great democratic society built on (1) laws, (2) the Constitution, and (3) a devotion to truth.

Jerry Falwell, *Textbooks in Public
Schools: A Disgrace and Concern to America* (1979)

Directory of Organizations and Associations

5

American Association of Christian Schools
4500 Selsa Road
Blue Springs MO 64015
(816) 795-7709
Fax (816) 795-7709

The association represents the interests of Protestant Christian schools. It provides teacher certification and classroom materials, publishes an annual directory of member schools, and helps lobby on behalf of its school members.

American Atheists
P.O. Box 2117
Austin TX 78768
(512) 458-1244
Fax (512) 467-9525

Relatively small group that opposes the use of any public funds or the provision of tax exemptions for the support of religion. The group opposes any religious observations in the schools.

American Center for Law and Justice
1000 Centerville Turnpike
P.O. Box 64429
Virginia Beach VA 23467
(804) 579-2489
Fax (804) 579-2836

Conservative public interest law firm specializing in religious issues such as freedom of expression for religious individuals. Originally established by Pat Robertson.

American Civil Liberties Union (ACLU)
132 West 43d Street
New York NY 10036
(212) 944-9800
Fax (212) 869-9065

Often derided by conservatives as a liberal, radical, or even communist organization, the ACLU is in fact much harder to label. Because of its absolutist support of First Amendment rights, including the right to free speech, the ACLU often supports unpopular minority views. In some cases, the ACLU position may seem "against" religion while in other cases it may seem to support religion. The ACLU is actively involved in religion in the schools issues, including the recitation of prayers in the schools.

American Coalition for Traditional Values
139 C Street SE
Washington DC 20003
(202) 547-8570

Founded in 1983 by conservative religious leaders Jerry Falwell, James Dobson, Jimmy Swaggert, and others, the organization has been headed from the start by Tim LaHaye, one of the nation's foremost conservative critics of public school curriculums. The group's stated aim is to reestablish traditional moral values, and the group supports a return of religion to the public schools. The organization has been a vocal proponent of a constitutional amendment to allow prayer in public schools.

Americans United for the Separation of Church and State
1816 Jefferson Parkway NW
Washington DC 20036
(202) 466-3234
Fax (202) 466-2587

Nationally prominent organization that supports the separation of church and state. The organization supports exclusion of organized prayer and Bible reading from the public schools and is against state support of religious schools. Currently headed by the Reverend Barry W. Lynn, Americans United, together with the ACLU and several conservative religious groups (with whom Americans United often disagrees), helped enact the Religious Freedom Restoration Act, which sought to limit the extent to which governments could limit an individual's religious expression.

Anti-Defamation League of B'nai B'rith (ADL)
823 UN Plaza
New York NY 10017
(212) 490-2525
Fax (212) 867-0779

The Anti-Defamation League was founded in 1913 "to stop the defamation of the Jewish people [and] to secure justice and fair treatment for all citizens alike." The ADL investigates and fights various hate groups, including the Ku Klux Klan and the American Nazis. The group is a vocal proponent of separation of church and state to protect minority rights. Accordingly, it opposes organized prayer and religious displays in the public schools and state support of private religious schools.

Campus Crusade for Christ International
100 Sunport Lane
Orlando FL 32809
(407) 826-2000

Conservative Christian organization that promotes Bible study and religious activity on college campuses. The group is also involved in promoting religious clubs and activities in high schools.

Christian Advocates Serving Evangelism (CASE)
P.O. Box 64429
Virginia Beach VA 23457
(804) 523-7239
Fax (804) 523-7546

A public interest law firm headed by Jay Sekulow. CASE is dedicated to expanding the opportunities for religious expression in many areas of public life, including the public schools. Notably, CASE was successful in the court case *Board of Education of the Westside Community Schools v. Mergens,* in which the Supreme Court held that voluntary student Bible clubs on school premises do not violate the establishment clause.

Christian Coalition
1801 Sarah Drive, Suite L
Chesapeake VA 23320
(804) 424-2630
Fax (804) 424-9068

Formed by evangelist Pat Robertson in 1989 as a Christian political advocacy group, the Christian Coalition soon gained enough membership to become a national political force with the ability to influence both political opinion and legislation. Under the direction of Ralph Reed, the organization grew rapidly, enlisting more than a million members. Since Reed's departure the group has continued its politically active agenda. The group lends its support to candidates who support traditional family values as defined by the group, including more religion in the public schools. The group distributes a "congressional scorecard" to both the press and its membership, rating candidates' positions on the issues.

Christian Crusade
P.O. Box 977
Tulsa OK 74102
(918) 438-4234
Fax (918) 438-4235

Although primarily known for its right-wing political stances, the Christian Crusade is also concerned with promoting conservative family values, including a return of religion to the public schools.

Coalition for Religious Freedom
5817 Dawes Avenue
Alexandria VA 22311

Advocacy organization that is opposed to attempts to limit or exclude organized prayer and other types of religious expression from the public schools.

Concerned Women for America (CWA)
370 L'Enfant Promenade, Suite 800
Washington DC 20024
(202) 488-7000
Fax (202) 488-0806

Founded by Beverly LaHaye (wife of Tim LaHaye, prominent opponent of secular humanism), the Washington-based CWA is a conservative organization that supports grassroots efforts by conservative Christian groups nationwide. Although once identified primarily as anti–Equal Rights Amendment, the group now has a very wide focus, including assisting parents who wish to challenge textbooks. The group also backs conservative Christians who are interested in serving on local school boards in order to restore religion to the public schools.

Eagle Forum
P.O. Box 618
Alton IL 62002
(618) 462-5415
Fax (618) 462-8909

Founded by Phyllis Schlafly, a Roman Catholic strongly opposed to abortion, the group originally focused on opposing legalized abortion but has since expanded its concerns to other issues involving traditional and family values, including opposing sex education in the public schools.

Family Research Council
700 13th Street, Suite 500
Washington DC 20005
(202) 393-2100
Fax (202) 393-2134

Conservative research organization interested in promoting traditional Christian values. Affiliated with James Dobson's Focus on the Family, the group provides research to political leaders, government, and the press.

Focus on the Family
420 North Cascade Avenue
Colorado Springs CO 80903
(719) 473-4020
Fax (719) 473-9751

An arm of James Dobson's radio ministry, Focus on the Family publishes several magazines, including *Teachers in Focus*, which explores family-related topics from a Christian perspective.

Freedom from Religion Foundation
P.O. Box 750
Madison WI 53701
(606) 256-8900
Fax (606) 256-1116

This group includes various freethinkers, including atheists and agnostics. The group opposes the use of public funds for religious purposes and is also opposed to organized prayer and other religious observances in the public schools.

John Birch Society
P.O. Box 8040
Appleton, WI 54913
(414) 749-3780
Fax (414) 749-3785

The grandfather of many right-wing groups, the John Birch Society was primarily an anti-Communist group. Named for a slain missionary, the group, led by its founder Robert Welch, called for the impeachment of Chief Justice Earl Warren after the Supreme Court outlawed organized prayer in the public schools.

Ku Klux Klan, Knights of the (KKK)
P.O. Box 222
Harrison, AR 72601
(501) 427-3414
Fax (501) 427-3414

The Klu Klux Klan is made up of a number of related groups, all using the name Klan and the trappings of the traditional Klan. The modern Klan was patterned after an earlier group that was formed to battle Reconstruction and freed slaves after the Civil War. The KKK is generally anti-Black, antisemitic, and anti-Catholic. Although more famous for parading in white hooded outfits and for burning crosses, the Klansmen most recently gained notoriety for erecting a cross on public land as a Christmas display. The Supreme Court decided that this cross had to be removed not because it was erected by the Klan but because its positioning on public property was in violation of the establishment clause. The Klan also supports the return of prayer to the public schools.

Liberty Federation
P.O. Box 2000
Lynchburg, VA 24506
(804) 582-7310

The Moral Majority was founded by the Reverend Jerry Falwell in 1979 as a political organization to represent the rights of conservative Christians. The organization was very interested in what was viewed as family values issues, including prayer in the public schools. During the early 1980s, the Moral Majority was perhaps the most powerful conservative Christian political group. By 1987, however, the organization was in serious decline, in the wake of scandals involving other evangelists such as Jimmy Swaggert and Jim Bakker. The organization was also investigated by the IRS. Falwell's Liberty Federation is the successor to the Moral Majority but has kept a much lower profile than its predecessor.

Liberty Lobby
300 Independence AUSE
Washington DC 20003
(202) 546-5611

Conservative group that lobbies for a return to what it views as traditional American values. Although the group supports conservative issues, it also supports the separation of church and state.

Moral Majority. *See* Liberty Federation

National Association of Evangelicals
P.O. Box 28
Wheaton IL 60189
(708) 665-0500
Fax (708) 665-8575

An umbrella group for fundamentalist churches and organizations that functions in the same way as the National Council of Churches. The group claims a membership of over 50,000 churches in the United States, including many leading evangelical churches. The organization is politically influential at both the local and national levels, and presidential candidates normally make an address at the association's national meeting. The group has often supported politicians who support religion in the schools, including a constitutional amendment to return organized prayers and Bible reading to the public schools.

National Legal Foundation
6477 College Park Square, Suite 306
Virginia Beach VA 23464
(804) 424-4242
Fax (804) 420-0855

Conservative public interest law firm that assists litigants in the area of religious freedom and religious expression, including cases that deal with religion in the schools. Originally founded by Pat Robertson, the group has assisted in many religion in the schools cases.

People for the American Way
2000 M Street NW, Suite 400
Washington DC 20036
(202) 467-4999
Fax (202) 293-2672

Liberal group that supports cultural pluralism and freedom of expression. The group frequently opposes actions by conservative groups in matters of religion in the schools. The group publishes an annual "Attacks on the Freedom to Learn," which details the year's attempts to challenge textbooks and library materials because of supposedly immoral content. The challenges are most often from conservative groups or parents who object to their sexual content, lack of religiosity, or moral relativism.

Traditional Values Coalition
P.O. Box 940
Anaheim CA 92815-0940
(714) 520-0300

Political group that promotes "traditional values" in American society. The group is currently supporting the Religious Equality Amendment that would recognize the rights of all Americans to express their religious beliefs in public places such as the schools. The group also supports prayer in public schools and is opposed to sex education, believing that to be a parental responsibility.

U.S. Catholic Conference
3211 4th Street West
Washington DC 20017
(202) 541-3000
Fax (202) 541-3322

Roman Catholic bishop's group that often voices an opinion on educational matters, especially those affecting parochial schools. The group recently endorsed the concept of parental rights, including "school choice."

Selected Print Resources 6

The works listed in this chapter are divided into two categories. The first lists both popular and scholarly books that deal with the topic of religion in the schools or separation of church and state. The second lists both law journal articles and newspaper articles dealing specifically with religion in the schools. Law journals are normally available only at law school libraries or law libraries at local courthouses (sometimes not open to the public). Some law review articles are available on the Internet. See Chapter 7 for a description of Internet legal research sites.

Books

Ahlstrom, Sydney E. *A Religious History of the American People.* New Haven, CT: Yale University Press, 1972.

Historical account of American religious practice and American churches from colonial times until 1970, including the development and application of the doctrine of separation of church and state and late twentieth century Supreme Court cases dealing with religion in the schools.

Allen, Leslie H., ed. *Bryan and Darrow at Dayton.* New York: Russel and Russel, 1925.

Contemporary account of the famous Scopes trial pitting William Jennings Bryan against Clarence Darrow. The trial ended in the conviction of John Scopes, a high school biology teacher, for teaching Darwin's theory of evolution in defiance of a Tennessee statute. Includes original source material, including a partial trial transcript.

Alley, Robert S. *The Supreme Court on Church and State.* New York: Oxford University Press, 1988.

A collection of lightly edited U.S. Supreme Court cases on the separation of church and state, most of which involve religion in the schools. The author also provides analyses of the areas. This is an excellent reference for the full text of the most important court cases up until the mid-1980s.

Barton, Charles D. *America: To Pray or Not to Pray.* Aledo, TX: Wallbuilders, 1989.

The book chronicles what the author perceives as problems in American society that resulted from the ending of organized prayer in the public schools. The author argues that prayer must be returned to the schools before these ills will reverse themselves.

Beggs, David W. III, and R. Bruch McQuigg. *America's Schools and Churches: Partners in Conflict.* Bloomington: Indiana University Press, 1965.

This is a dated but useful treatise on cases involving challenges to religion in the schools and a good source concerning the hysteria that accompanied the Supreme Court's decision banning organized prayer in public school classrooms.

Bollier, David. *Liberty and Justice for Some: Defending a Free Society from the Radical Right's Holy War on Democracy.* Washington, D.C.: People for the American Way, 1982.

In a vigorous defense of the doctrine of separation of church and state, Bollier criticizes what he views as the religious right's attack on pluralistic society and protection of minority rights in the United States.

Butts, R. Freeman. *Religion, Education, and the First Amend-*

ment: The Appeal to History. Washington, D.C.: People for the American Way, 1986.

Historical background on the separation of church and state in the schools from a strict separationist viewpoint. The book makes the argument that the founders' initial notion was for the strict separation of church and state and that that original intent should be reflected in today's public schools.

Carter, Stephen L. *The Culture of Disbelief: How American Law and Politics Trivialize Religious Devotion.* New York: Basic Books, 1993.

General overview of the secularization of American society, including the secularization of the public schools. The author argues that attempts by politicians and the courts to protect religious diversity have actually resulted in a secular public sector that is counter to the wishes of both the founders and a majority of today's citizens.

Cord, Robert L. *Separation of Church and State: Historical Fact and Current Fiction.* New York: Lambeth Press, 1982.

Scholarly examination of the Supreme Court's jurisprudence in the area of separation of church and state, including the Court's controversial decision on religion in the schools. The author believes that the original intent of the founding fathers was not to have strict separation and that the Supreme Court has been selective in quoting Madison and Jefferson and has repeatedly ignored sources that prove that the founders never intended a complete separation. The author, a law professor, makes a strong case, but the tone of the book is often sour.

Costannzo, Joseph S. J. *This Nation under God: Church, State and Schools in America.* New York: Herder and Herder, 1963.

An interesting polemical treatment of the subject of religion in the schools by a Catholic priest. The author writes that many of the Supreme Court's decisions in the area of church-state separation are clearly wrong and not constitutionally mandated.

Data Research. *1997 Deskbook Encyclopedia of American School Law.* Rosemont, MN: Data Research, Inc., 1997.

Annual encyclopedia that compiles the decisions in both state and federal court cases dealing with school law. A chapter on freedom of religion collects and describes court decisions dealing with religion in the schools. Because it is updated annually, this book provides good current materials for researchers.

Dolbeare, Kenneth, and Phillip E. Hammond. *The School Prayer Decisions.* Chicago: University of Chicago Press, 1971.

Scholarly work that examines a community's disregard of the ban on prayer in the public schools. The authors put this defiance into the historical perspective of the many U.S. Supreme Court cases on the subject.

Douglas, William O. *The Bible and the Schools.* Boston: Little Brown, 1966.

Although now dated, this volume is interesting because it was written by one of the Supreme Court justices who took part in many of the opinions. Justice Douglas, a religious man but also a protector of minority rights, examines the pros and cons of excluding religion from the schools.

Elwell, Walter A., ed. *Evangelical Dictionary of Theology.* Grand Rapids, MI: Baker Book House, 1984.

General reference work with brief entries on both people, doctrine, and religious practices. Although the entries are rather brief, the coverage is comprehensive. This volume would be most useful to those who may be unfamiliar with religious terms.

Engel, David E., ed. *Religion in Public Education: Problems and Prospects.* New York: Paulist Press, 1974.

Collection of essays on religion in the public schools, mainly from a Catholic perspective. The essays support the view that religion should not be excluded from public life but that at the same time provision should be made for members of religious minorities. The volume includes a useful bibliography, although now dated.

Flowers, Ronald B. *That Godless Court?* Louisville, KY: Westminster John Knox Press, 1994.

Scholarly treatment of U.S. Supreme Court decisions on church-state relations. The discussion includes the topics of government aid to church-supported schools and prayer in the public schools. The author is a strict separationist, although the title might suggest the opposite.

Frankel, F. Marvin. *Faith and Freedom: Religious Liberty in America.* New York: Hill and Wang, 1994.

The author, a famous former federal judge in Manhattan, writes on the issue of religious liberty, including religion in the schools. Frankel is a strict separationist although he writes on the value of religion in American life.

Geisler, Norman, A. F. Brooke, and Mark Keough. *The Creator in the Classroom: 'Scopes II,' the 1981 Arkansas Creation-Evolution Trial.* Milford, MI: Mott Media, 1982.

Detailed examination of *McClean v. Arkansas* (1981), in which the Arkansas law mandating that the biblical account of creation be taught in the schools was declared unconstitutional. The book provides an interesting treatment of the parties behind the lawsuit.

Goldberg, George. *Church, State, and the Constitution.* Washington, DC: Regency Gateway, 1987.

Although it includes a number of areas under the separation-of-church-and-state umbrella, most of the book pertains to the issue of religion in the schools. The author makes no attempt at a balanced view and blames the separationists for what he sees as the "judicial nonsense" of removing God and religion from the public schools.

Gould, Stephen Jay. *Ever Since Darwin.* New York: Norton Press, 1977.

Contemporary examination of the theory of evolution. Gould, an award-winning science writer, makes a compelling case for evolution and the continued teaching of evolution as the preferred explanation of human creation.

Hook, Sidney, B. F. Skinner, and Isaac Asimov. *Humanist Manifestos I and II.* New York: Prometheus Books, 1973.

The bible of the humanists, these works by three of the twentieth century's leading minds are anathema to conservative critics who believe that they promote a godless society. This is the book that spurred several Christian writers to write antihumanist tracts.

Jorstad, Erling. *The Christian Right, 1981–1988: Prospects for the Post-Reagan Era.* Lewiston, NY: Edwin Mellen, 1987.

The book discusses the political ties of conservative Christians and their efforts to promote their cause through the political process. Although the material is now somewhat dated, some insight is provided into the educational and social goals of the Christian right.

Kurland, Phillip B., ed. *Church and State: The Supreme Court and the First Amendment.* Chicago: University of Chicago Press, 1975.

Scholarly legal essays drawn from the University of Chicago's annual *Supreme Court Review,* which always draws contributions from the nation's leading constitutional scholars. Although the essays are dated, they provide excellent scholarly analysis of the school prayer cases of the 1960s and 1970s that are still "good law." The material is scholarly and may be inaccessible to those without some legal background.

LaHaye, Tim. *The Battle For The Mind.* Old Tappan, NJ: Fleming H. Revell, 1980.

LaHaye, a vigorous critic of secular humanism, argues that the real battle for America is taking place in the public schools, pitting the pious against the forces of secular humanism. The author calls for a return of God and religion to the public schools.

———. *The Race for the Twentieth Century.* Nashville, TN: Thomas Nelson, 1986.

LaHaye outlines his theory that America is witnessing a race between secular humanism and conservative Christianity for the hearts and minds of American youth.

Levy, Leonard W. *Constitutional Problems in Church-State Relations: A Symposium.* New York: DaCapo Press, 1971.

Reprint of 1966 issue of *Northwestern Law Review* dedicated to essays on the separation of church and state including religion in the schools. Although the material is dated, the essays provide a sound and scholarly introduction to the legal underpinnings of the Supreme Court's establishment clause and free exercise clause jurisprudence. The essays may be difficult for those unfamiliar with legal scholarship.

———. *The Establishment Clause: Religion and the First Amendment.* Macmilliam, 1986.

Levy, one of the foremost First Amendment scholars and a strict separationist, illustrates both original intent of the founders and current application of the First Amendment in a number of contexts, including religious practices in the schools. This is must reading for understanding the First Amendment.

Lynn, Barry, Marc D. Stern, and Oliver Thomas. *The Right to Religious Liberty: The Basic ACLU Guide to Religious Rights.* 2d ed. New York: ACLU, 1995.

The American Civil Liberties Union handbook covering the role of religion in many facets of public life, including the public schools. The handbook is arranged in question-and-answer format and is referenced to the many relevant court cases.

Manwaring, David R. *Render unto Caesar and Religion.* Chicago: University of Chicago Press, 1962.

Scholarly examination of the legal disputes that arose when Jehovah's Witnesses refused to recite the pledge of allegiance in the public schools. Very detailed treatment of an issue that is now largely forgotten.

Matriscana, Carly, and Roger Oakland. *The Evolution Conspiracy.* Eugene, OR: Harvest House, 1991.

This book presents a conservative Christian defense of the biblical account of creation and criticizes evolution as an unsubstantiated theory. The author writes that educators and judges have colluded to exclude religion from the schools.

McCay, Mary, ed. *Equal Separation: Understanding the Religion Clauses of the First Amendment.* Westport, CT: Greenwood, 1990.

Essays based on a panel discussion by scholars in the area of separation of church and state. The essays represent both separationist and accommodationist viewpoints and the work provides a balanced view of the issues.

McWhirter, Darien A. *The Separation of Church and State.* Exploring the Constitution series. Phoenix, AZ: Oryx, 1994.

Well-written, current reference text that presents both analysis of the area and heavily edited U.S. Supreme Court cases. Although the book includes many topics in addition to education, many of the cases presented come from the religion in the schools area.

Menendez, Albert J. *School Prayer and Other Religious Issues in American Public Education: A Bibliography.* New York: Garland, 1985.

Very thorough bibliography on religion in the schools to 1985. Although now dated, this work provides a starting point for serious scholarship in the area of religion in the schools.

Numbers, Ronald L., ed. *Creation-Evolution Debates.* Hamden, CT: Garland, 1995.

This volume reproduces original source documents from the 1920s defending and attacking the theory of evolution. The collection includes an essay by William Jennings Bryan, the attorney who won the Scopes trial, upholding Tennessee's antievolution law.

Pfeffer, Leo. *God, Caesar, and the Constitution: The Court As Referee of Church-State Confrontation.* Boston: Beacon, 1975.

A leading separationist scholar, Pfeffer describes the role of the Supreme Court in umpiring the line between church and state, including the role of the Court in protecting minority interests in the public schools. Although the text is somewhat dated, the analysis remains perceptive.

Provenzo, Eugene F., Jr. *Religious Fundamentalism and American Education: The Battle for the Public Schools:* Albany, NY: SUNY Press, 1990.

This paperback book examines a number of issues concerning religion in the schools, including classroom materials, the teaching of creationism, and school prayer. The tone is generally critical of conservative Christian beliefs.

Rice, Charles E. *The Supreme Court and Public Prayer.* New York: Fordham University Press, 1964.

This book presents the argument, from the Catholic viewpoint, that the Supreme Court's school prayer decisions were incorrect and that prayer and other religious practices should be returned to the schools.

Sherrow, Victoria. *Separation of Church and State.* New York: Franklin Watts, 1991.

Well-researched and accessible work on separation of church and state issues, including the topic of religion in the schools. The author gives a number of interesting insights, but there is little legal analysis. Appropriate for the high school audience.

Stokes, Anson Phelps, and Leo Pfeffer. *Church and State in the United States*. Westport, CT: Greenwood, 1964.

The basic scholarly volume on church and state relations including the school prayer cases. Although the text is now dated, this text remains a basic reference in the area because of the scholarly approach.

Tribe, Laurence H. *God Save This Honorable Court: How the Choice of Justices Can Change Our Lives*. New York: Random House, 1985.

Written by Laurence Tribe, Harvard Law School professor and leading constitutional scholar, this popular book illustrates how individual personalities on the Supreme Court have influenced the Court's decisions, including those dealing with religion in the schools.

Utter, Glenn H., and John W. Storey. *The Religious Right: A Reference Handbook*. Santa Barbara, CA: ABC-CLIO, 1995.

Handbook on the religious right with an emphasis on conservative Christians. The volume is a current sourcebook for studying the many individuals and groups composing the religious right. The book describes both the theological development of the religious right and their political agenda, including the return of religion to the public schools.

Scholarly Articles

Cohen, Joseph C., Jr. **Fundamentalist Christians, the Public Schools and the Religion Clauses.** *Denver University Law Review* 66 (Winter 1989): 289–333.

The author argues that demands for changes in the public schools by the Religious Right are incompatible with the U.S. Constitution, Supreme Court precedents, and traditional notions of the role of the public schools in American life. The author argues that the Religious Right criticizes the courts, yet at the same time uses the courts to further its agenda of bringing religion into the schools. Although Christians should be concerned over the lack of teaching about religion in the schools, the public schools should not try to accommodate all the demands of the Religious Right.

Dent, George W. Jr. **Of God and Caesar: The Free Exercise Rights of Public School Students.** Symposium: Religion and the Public Schools after *Lee v. Weisman. Case Western Reserve Law Review* (Spring 1993): 707–752.

This article supports an accommodationist view of religion in the schools. The United States is committed to providing every child with a free education and has chosen to do so by running free public schools. However, according to the author, the schools often denigrate religion, especially traditional religion, inflicting pain on religious people. The government needs to accommodate the needs of religious Americans so families are not forced to choose between education and faith.

Durso, Keith E. **The Voluntary School Prayer Debate: A Separationist Perspective.** *Journal of Church and State* 36 (Winter 1994): 79–96.

The separationist viewpoint that organized prayer should be excluded from the public schools is discussed in this article. The author also laments that prayer has become a political football that has obscured the deeper issues in the debate over religion in the schools. The author argues that organized prayer should be excluded because it always has the potential to offend students and their families who are not in the religious majority.

Hall, Timothy L. **Sacred Solemnity: Civic Prayer, Civil Communion, and the Establishment Clause.** *Iowa Law Review* 79 (October 1993): 35–93.

This lengthy article looks at the future of the religion in the schools issue. The author suggests that the courts will drop their attempt to find a grand organizing principle that will guide their decisions. He argues that the courts will instead develop a number of subdoctrines that can be used to judge the legality of specific issues and that the focus of the courts should not be on the role of government as the manipulator of religious belief, but on protecting minority views and promoting civil fellowship.

Hamre, James S. **The Creationist-Evolutionist Debate and the Public Schools.** *Journal of Church and State* 33 (Autumn 1991): 765–784.

In this article dealing with the teaching of creationism in the public schools, the author suggests that, although the Supreme Court has struck down laws authorizing the teaching of creationism, the issue will continue to be debated because a large number of religious Americans believe that creationism is correct. The author predicts that the battle between evolutionists and creationists will shift from the national to the local stage.

Layton, Donald H. **Religion and the Politics of Education: An Introduction.** *Education and Urban Society* 28, no. 3 (May 1996): 275–278.

The impact of organized religion and various religious groups on the public schools, which groups are actively trying to influence curriculum in the schools, and the legal aspects of these efforts are all discussed in this article. The author is critical of the motives of some of these groups who wish to impose their views on the public school curriculum.

O'Neil, Michael R. **Government's Denigration of Religion: Is God the Victim of Discrimination in Our Public Schools?** *Pepperdine Law Review* 21 (January 1994): 477–552.

The author argues that the courts have discriminated against religion—that while nonbelievers are protected against religious arguments, the religious get no protection from ideas that their families find offensive. The author writes that one does not have to be a "radical fundamentalist" to believe in the precepts of one's faith or to reject evolution as fact. The author argues that the government has gone well beyond being neutral in this controversy and is actively antireligious.

Sorenson, Gail. **Religion and American Public Education: Conservative Religious Agendas and the U.S. Constitution.** *Education and Urban Society* 28, no. 3 (May 1996): 293–307.

The article examines the relationship between religious groups and public schools in the United States. The author argues that there is no conspiracy by the government or teachers to exclude religion from the public schools or to indoctrinate children to discriminate against religion.

Stone, Geoffrey R. **The Equal Access Controversy: The Religion Clauses and the Meaning of 'Neutrality'.** Symposium: Freedom of Association. *Northwestern University Law Review* 81 (Fall 1986): 168–173.

The author argues against equal access for religious activities and clubs in the public schools. The author rejects the notion that public schools are like public parks where access to religion should be tolerated. He argues that the movement toward allowing religious clubs is not neutral at all but promotes religion.

Yerby, Winton E. III. **Toward Religious Neutrality in the Public School Curriculum.** *University of Chicago Law Review* 56 (Spring 1989): 899–934.

The focus in many of the court cases involving religion in the schools has been wrong, and the courts should not judge schools' actions to see if students are being indoctrinated, this author argues. Further, nonreligion can actually be antireligion. The author argues that the schools should strive for curriculum that allows a diversity of religious views.

Selected Nonprint Resources

7

This chapter contains three sections. The first describes audiotapes dealing with religion in the schools or related matters. The second section lists Internet resources for researching religion in the schools and provides a brief description for online searching and a list of selected web sites. The third section includes videotapes on the same subjects.

Audiotapes

Is Science Religious?
Type: audiocassette
Length: 60 minutes
Cost: $5.00
Source: Reasons To Believe
          P.O. Box 5978
          Pasadena, CA 9117
          (818) 335-1480

Produced by an organization affiliated with the Campus Crusade for Christ International and the National Association of Evangelicals, this tape suggests that creation science is both compatible with traditional biblical teachings and scientifically valid. The tape consists of a discussion between a critic and a defender of creation science.

May It Please the Court
Type: audiocassette
Length: 8 hours
Cost: $45.00
Source: W. W. Norton
          800 Keystone Industrial Park
          Scranton, PA 18512
          (800) 223-2584

Original recordings of important twentieth century Supreme Court cases, including the attorneys arguing before the Court and questioning by the Supreme Court justices. The set includes both *Abington v. Schempp*, the 1963 case that struck down Bible-reading in the schools, and *Edwards v. Aguillard*, the 1987 case that struck down Louisiana's "balanced treatment" law that allowed equal time for the teaching of evolution and "creation science" in the state's public schools.

Internet Resources

The Internet contains a rich assortment of resources for researching the subject of religion in the schools. Many individuals as well as organizations maintain web sites devoted to this topic. Religion in the schools is often discussed under the heading "separation of church and state." Although some web sites listed contain very recent material, other sites are seldom updated. Unfortunately, web site addresses change frequently. All of the addresses listed here were active when this book was written, but if the listed address does not work, try using the name of the organization or the name of the site with your browser to find the new address.

Religion in the Schools Sites

The following selected web sites include material on religion in the schools. Some of the sites contain primary source materials while others contain individual opinions. Most of the sources advocate either strict separation or accommodation, although a few provide a more balanced view. Accordingly, users should be aware that many of the sites provide only material advocating one side of the issue or the other.

Americans United for the Separation of Church and State
http://www.netplexgroup.com/americansunited@au.org

This organization is one of the more visible proponents of maintaining a strict separation of church and state in all areas of public life. The organization's web site reflects this approach, but it is a good source of basic material on church/state matters.

Baptist Joint Committee on Public Affairs
http://www.erols.com/bjcpa/index.htm

This web site is a good source of recent activity, including court cases, concerning religion in the schools. The organization is a defender of the separation of church and state. There is coverage of current and future issues, including vouchers and proposed constitutional amendments dealing with religion in the schools.

Baylor University
http://www.baylor.edu/~Church_State/

Sponsored by the Truett Seminary on the campus of Baylor University in Texas, the site has an extensive section on the separation of church and state, including materials that relate to religion in the schools.

Christian Coalition
http://www.cc.org/search2html

This is a large web site that contains material on a number of issues, including many pertaining to religion in the schools. The Christian Coalition is an advocacy group that supports accommodation of religion in the schools. The site is so large that it contains its own search engine that will help the user navigate through the large library of materials.

Christian Science Monitor
http://www.csmonitor.com/csmonitor/index.html

This site is maintained by the *Christian Science Monitor* and operated by the Christian Science church. The site contains information on separation of church and state issues.

First Amendment Cyber-Tribune
http://www.trib.com/FACT/

Award-winning site sponsored by the Caspar, Wyoming, *Star-*

Tribune, it includes much separation of church and state material along with other First Amendment materials. The site contains documents, Supreme Court rulings, and First Amendment information. This is one of the very best sites for finding current information, as it is updated on a weekly basis.

National Academy of Sciences
http://www.nas.edu/readingroom/books/evolution98/

This portion of the large NAS web site contains the full text of their publication "Teaching About Evolution and the Nature of Science." This document provides a rich source of material on evolution and also contains material on the legal aspects of the issue. The full text of the publication can be downloaded.

On the Separation of Church and State
http://www.mindspring.com/~edge/separate.html

This site contains a variety of quotations from treaties and state constitutions and Thomas Jefferson and other prominent individuals. The quotes generally support a strong separationist view of the constitutional protections.

Papers Dealing with the Relationship of Church and State and Religious Liberty
http://www.members.aol.com/larrypahl/poli-sci.htm

Operated by Larry Pahl, this is a most interesting site for researchers. There are search engines that search through 150 newspapers for articles on both religious liberty and the establishment clause. The site contains many academic papers on church-state issues; the articles generally support the separationist view. There are also links to a good number of related web sites.

People for the American Way
http://www.pfaw.org

The site is maintained by an organization opposed to the Religious Right and the web site's content reflects this view. The site includes a discussion of prayer and religious activities in the schools, attempts at censorship, teaching of creationism, and vouchers.

Quotations Concerning the Separation of Church and State
http://www.southwind.net/cdoc/jproj/csquotes.html

A rich assortment of quotes, from a wide variety of sources—especially from colonial times—can be found at this site. It supplies quotes that support the accommodationist view that religion should not be excluded from the schools and other facets of public life.

Rutherford Institute
http://www.rutherford.org

This site is maintained by a conservative political organization that has been involved in a number of high-profile legal cases, including the Paula Jones case against President Clinton. The institute is especially interested in religious liberty issues.

Separation of Church and State
http://www.louisville.edu/~tnpete01/church/index.htm

A good place to start research; although the site itself is not extensive, it contains a listing of links to other church-state separation web sites. The site was created and is maintained by three individuals who advocate strict separation of church and state. However, it also contains much politically neutral source material. Topics include an overview of the debate, the case for separation of church and state, what the founders believed about separation, answering the religious right, misquoting by the religious right, the case against government-sponsored prayer, the case against school vouchers, important establishment cases, timely articles, and separationist documents. The site also includes "links of importance" that also advocate the separationist view.

Internet Legal Resources

Many of the disputes involving religion in the schools have made their way to the courts and more than a few have progressed all the way to the Supreme Court. Although legal research was once difficult for laypersons, the Internet has made the job considerably easier. Court cases are available on several web sites. These sites can be searched by case name or subject.

Find Law
http://www.findlaw.com/casecode/

This is an easy-to-use site that provides access to both current and historical material. The site has an easy-to-use search engine to help with research. The site also allows users to access law review articles and to search them by subject.

GPO Access
http://www.gpoaccesso.gov/su_docs/aces/aaces002.html

The official web site of the federal government publications office provides access to both federal laws and court cases. The site contains its own search engine that can be used to look for specific items or topics. Use the first box to find the file "Supreme Court cases," then use the search box to find a particular case or topic. The Supreme Court cases can be downloaded in full or in summary form.

'Lectric Law Library
http://www.lectlaw.com

This is a rewarding site that provides a vast amount of legal information that can be easily accessed. The site is organized as a "library" with various "reading rooms" that contain different subjects. Supreme Court cases can be accessed here. This award-winning site also has several less serious nooks and crannies that can provide some diversion.

Legal Information Institute
http://www.law.cornell.edu

This site, maintained by Cornell University Law School, is one of the premier electronic law libraries available. It contains both recent and historical U.S. Supreme Court cases. The site has its own search engine that can help pinpoint material. The full text of court cases is available and can be downloaded in text or in word processing format. This site contains useful links to other legal research sites.

Villanova Law On-Line
http://vls.Law.vill.edu

This site provides an excellent source of legal materials, including full-text legal cases. The site has its own easy-to-use search engine and is somewhat easier to use than many of the other legal sites.

Videotapes

Books Our Children Read
Type: 1/2" videocassette
Length: 28 minutes
Cost: $129.00
Source: Insight Media
2162 Broadway
New York, NY 10024
(212) 721-6316

This film examines book banning and censorship of classroom material in a small Ohio town. Parents, teachers, and students express their opinions about the process. The program illustrates that censorship of classroom material is one of the most contentious issues involving religion in the schools and has the potential to create serious divisions in a school or even an entire community.

Creation and the Supreme Court
Type: 1/2" videocassette
Length: 120 minutes
Cost: $10.00
Source: Reasons to Believe
P.O. Box 5978
Pasadena, CA 91117
(818) 335-1480

The film provides a critical examination of the Supreme Court's decision striking down Arkansas' law allowing the teaching of creationism in the public schools. The film presents the background and justifications for creation science and argues that creationism should be taught in biology classes in the public schools.

Darwinism on Trial
Type: 1/2" videocassette
Length: 120 minutes
Cost: $30.00
Source: Reasons To Believe
P.O. Box 5978
Pasadena, CA 91117
(818) 335-1480

This film, based on work by the conservative Christian Philip

Johnson, upholds the biblical account of creation. Although many people believe that the battle to teach creationism rather than evolution ended with the Scopes trial in the 1920s, many Americans believe in the biblical account of the creation and reject evolution as an unproven theory. This tape provides a detailed and rational examination of creationism and attempts to revoke Darwinian science. The film does not claim to provide a balanced view of the topic.

Education and the Founding Fathers
Type: 1/2" videocassette
Length: 60 minutes
Cost: $20.00
Source: Wallbuilders
P.O. Box 397
Aledo, TX 76008
(817) 441-6044

Created by conservative Christian David Barton, the video presents the religious beliefs of several of the founding fathers, including George Washington, to support the idea that religion should be returned to the public schools. The film suggests that contemporary school curriculums should reflect the views of the founding fathers with more emphasis on biblical teachings.

Evolution: Science or Religion?
Type: 1/2" videocassette
Length: 30 minutes
Cost: $35.00
Source: Bible-Science Association, Inc.
P.O. Box 3320
Minneapolis, MN 55433
(800) 422-4253

Part of a tape series entitled "Origins," this video program discusses evolution from both a practical and theoretical perspective. The program explores the impact of Darwin and how evolution has shaped religious thinking in the twentieth century. The tape discusses how both creation science and evolution could be taught in the public schools.

First Amendment Freedoms
Type: 1/2" videocassette
Length: 30 minutes

Cost: $129.00
Source: Insight Media
             2162 Broadway
             New York, NY 10024
             (212) 721-6316

Interviews with political scientists and other constitutional experts about the status of religious freedom as guaranteed by the First Amendment. Although the film is primarily about freedom of religion, it also includes discussions about freedom of the press and the right to peaceable assembly.

For the People
Type: 1/2" videocassette
Length: 60 minutes
Cost: $89.95
Source: Films for the Humanities and Sciences
             P.O. Box 2053
             Princeton, NJ 08543-2053
             (800) 257-5126

This film discusses the impact of three important Supreme Court cases, including the Supreme Court's landmark school prayer case, *Engel v. Vitale*. The film explores the background of the school prayer case, the Court's rationale for the decision, and the consequences of the Court's banning of organized school prayer. The other two cases involve academic freedom and homosexual sodomy.

God and the Constitution
Type: 1/2" videocassette
Length: 60 minutes
Cost: $89.95
Source: Films for the Humanities and Sciences
             P.O. Box 2053
             Princeton, NJ 08543-2053
             (800) 257-5126

A part of the "In Search of the Constitution" series with Bill Moyers, the film presents Martin Marrty and Leonard Levy, two constitutional scholars specializing in religion in the schools, who discuss school prayer, religious symbols on public property including the schools, and tax-exempt status for religious institutions. The film attempts to give a balanced view of the topic.

Inherit the Wind
Type: 1/2" videocassette
Length: 130 minutes
Cost: $20.00
Source: Movies Unlimited
6736 Castro Avenue
Philadelphia, PA 19149
(800) 523-0823

1960 Hollywood version of the Scopes trial, pitting William Jennings Bryan and Clarence Darrow, with Spencer Tracy and Frederick March in the title roles. Although the film is compelling, it makes no attempt at being balanced. While Darrow is portrayed as a champion of reason, Bryan and his supporters are portrayed as ignorant religious fanatics.

Religion, Politics and Our Schools
Type: 1/2" videocassette
Length: 90 minutes
Cost: $70.00
Source: American Humanist Association
7 Hardwood Drive
Amhurst, NY 14226-0146
(716) 839-5080

This video presents a discussion of separation of church and state as it pertains to the public schools. The Humanist Association opposes the teaching of creationism and religious activity in the public schools and the film takes a proseparation stance.

Vista: A Battle for Public Education
Type: videocassette
Length: 11 minutes
Cost: $29.95
Source: People for the American Way
2000 M Street, NW
Suite 400
Washington, DC 20036
(202) 467-4999

This documentary describes a California town's reaction to a Religious Right takeover of a local school board. The film is an exposé of the fundamentalists and makes the case that they intend to infiltrate school boards across the country with the intent of restoring religious observances and to substitute Christian-oriented curriculums in place of the current offerings.

Glossary

affirmed In the practice of the appellate courts, the decree or order is declared valid and will stand as rendered in the lower court.

agnostic Person who is skeptical about the existence or nonexistence of God. An agnostic might argue that it is impossible to logically conclude that God either exists or doesn't exist because of lack of reliable evidence. An agnostic might also argue that it is likewise impossible to know the ultimate origin of the universe.

amicus curiae "Friend of the court." When a legal case is appealed from a trial court to an appeals court the judges do not hear witnesses but rely on trial transcripts and briefs submitted by the parties to the lawsuit. In important cases other persons or entities may file "friend of the court" (amicus curiae) briefs, urging the court to decide a case one way or another. Groups supporting or opposing religious activity in the schools often submit such briefs.

answer The formal written statement by a defendant responding to a civil complaint and setting forth the grounds for defense.

appeal A request made after a trial, asking another court (usually the court of appeals) to decide whether the trial was conducted properly. To make such a request is "to appeal" or "to take an appeal." One who appeals is called the appellant.

appellate About appeals. An appellate court has the power to review the judgment of another lower court or tribunal.

atheist Person who denies the existence of God or the existence of God's works on earth. This differs somewhat from a "freethinker," who believes only what appears rational and may have lost faith.

balanced curriculum, balanced treatment This term is used by religious educators to describe a school curriculum that presents both evolution and divine creation ("creationism") as equally plausible explanations of human origin. Only a few states have enacted laws requiring "balanced curriculums"; others have rejected such measures. Louisiana's balanced curriculum law was declared invalid by the U.S. Supreme Court in *Edwards, Governor of Louisiana v. Aguillard* (1986).

Bill of Rights First ten amendments to the U.S. Constitution. As originally drafted, the U.S. Constitution contained no list of individual rights and protections of citizens. Although the drafters argued that such protections were implicit in the document, a considerable number of prominent persons announced that they would not support ratification without such an explicit enumeration of guaranteed rights, freedoms, and protections. James Madison and other members of the Constitutional Convention debated various amendments, many of which concerned religious freedoms. These debates culminated in the familiar first ten amendments popularly known as the Bill of Rights. Once ratified by the original states they became part of the new Constitution in 1791. The Bill of Rights was originally interpreted to apply only to actions of the federal government, not to actions of state and local governments. Since about 1960, the courts have uniformly held that the Fourteenth Amendment applies the Bill of Rights to state and local governments as well.

Blaine Amendment Proposed but never-enacted constitutional amendment that would have specifically extended the establishment clause and free exercise clause of the First Amendment to the states. First proposed by James G. Blaine of Maine who later ran unsuccessfully for president, the amendment would have also prohibited any government aid to parochial schools. Although the amendment was brought before a number of Congresses in the late 1800s, it was never enacted. However, the U.S. Supreme Court ultimately extended these amendments to the states.

brief A written statement submitted by the lawyer for each side in a case that explains to the judge why the judge should decide the case or a particular part of a case in favor of that lawyer's client. When a legal case is appealed from a trial court to an appeals court the judges do not hear witnesses or evaluate evidence but rely on trial transcripts and briefs submitted by the parties to the lawsuit. A brief may be from a dozen to a hundred pages in length.

certiorari, writ of The U.S. Supreme Court hears appeals from federal courts and from state supreme courts. One or both parties must petition the court for a writ of certiorari, which orders the litigants to appear before the Court to argue the case. Of the thousands of writs submitted annually, the Court accepts fewer than one hundred cases that it deems most important.

chief judge   The judge who has primary responsibility for the administration of a court but also decides cases; chief judges are determined by seniority.

chief justice   The chief judge of the U.S. Supreme Court. The president has the power to appoint the chief justice, but once appointed, the chief justice, like other federal judges, serves for life.

common law   The legal system that originated in England and is now in use in the United States. It is based on judicial decisions rather than legislative action.

compelling interest test   A test formulated by the U.S. Supreme Court in applying the free exercise clause of the First Amendment to actual cases. The test is used to determine if a particular law is in violation of the First Amendment's protection of the free exercise of religion. Under the test, a law interfering with the person's free exercise of religion can only be applied against that person if the state demonstrates that the law furthers a compelling government interest that cannot be met by a less restrictive means. For example, a state law that requires all school-age children to attend secular public school and does not allow schooling in religious schools would be judged under the compelling interest test.

compulsory   Required. The courts have recognized that "compulsion" does not have to be overt or direct, but may be subtle and indirect. For example, a verbalized school prayer may be labeled voluntary. But the courts recognize that although a child is not being compelled to recite the prayer the recitation led by the teacher in the classroom amounts to subtle and indirect pressure.

compulsory education laws   Law requiring children over a certain age to attend school. These laws have caused a controversy with parents who wish to prevent their children from attending public school because they object to the secular atmosphere of public schools or because they prefer a school that also teaches religious principles.

concurring opinion   When more than one judge hears a case, one or more judges on the panel may agree with the result but not the logic contained in the majority opinion. This judge may write a concurring opinion explaining why he or she agrees with the decision but offering an alternate explanation for the result in the case. If there are a number of judges who agree with the concurring opinion they may "join" or adopt the concurrence. Alternately, they may write their own concurring opinions.

conscientious objector   Person who objects to military service or other government action on religious or moral grounds. The United States, like other nations, has long exempted conscientious objectors from combat duty in the armed forces.

counsel   Legal advice. Term used to refer to lawyers in a case.

counterclaim   A claim that a defendant makes against a plaintiff.

court   Government entity authorized to resolve legal disputes. Judges sometimes use "court" to refer to themselves in the third person, as in "the court has read the briefs."

creation science ("scientific creationism")   After the U.S. Supreme Court prohibited states from banning the teaching of evolution in *Epperson v. Arkansas* (1968), creationists started labeling their body of information supporting the biblical version of creation as "creation science." By so doing, the creationists—including those who founded the Creation Science Research Center and the Institute of Creation Research, both in California—hoped to establish a scientific underpinning for the biblical account of human origins. Creation science's adherents have enjoyed some limited success in getting a couple of states to incorporate their theories into school textbooks.

creationism   Belief that the biblical account of the creation in the book of Genesis is the one correct explanation of human origin. Some Christians, such as Pope John Paul, have surmised that the account in Genesis can be reconciled with the theory of evolution because the account is metaphorical rather than literal. Creationists who accept the biblical account literally also dispute the age of the earth, alleging that the earth is less ancient than scientists allege.

damages   Money paid by defendants to successful plaintiffs in civil cases to compensate the plaintiffs for their injuries.

default judgment   A judgment rendered because of the defendant's failure to answer or appear.

defendant   In a civil suit, the person complained against; in a criminal case, the person accused of the crime.

deist   A person who rejects the conception of a Supreme Being as the ruler and inspiration of man but still believes that there was a creator of the universe.

dicta   Language in a judicial opinion that is not directly relevant to deciding the case. The language amounts to the judge's observation about the state of the law. Because the language is not necessary to decide the case, the language has no value as precedent.

dismissed time   *See* release time.

dissent   When more than one judge hears a case, one or more judges may not agree with the opinion of the majority. The dissenter may simply state his or her dissent but more likely will write a dissenting opinion explaining why he or she disagrees with the logic and result of the majority opinion. If more than one judge dissents they may all "join" or adopt one dissenting opinion or they may pen their own dissenting opinions.

docket   A log containing brief entries of court proceedings. The cases that will be heard by a court are called its "docket." When a case is on the Supreme Court's docket it will be heard during the Court's next term.

due process   The due process clause of the Fifth Amendment of the U.S. Constitution guarantees that no person shall "be deprived of life, liberty, or property without due process of law." Procedural due process guarantees that before depriving anyone of liberty or property the government must provide them with a fair procedure, including notice and a hearing before a neutral fact finder. The Fourteenth Amendment to the Constitution also contains a due process clause, which states: "Nor shall any State deprive any person of life, liberty, or property, without due process of law."

en banc   "In the bench" or "full bench." Refers to court sessions with the entire membership of a court participating rather than the usual quorum. U.S. courts of appeals usually sit in panels of three judges but may expand to a larger number in certain cases. They are then said to be sitting en banc.

Equal Access Act of 1984   Federal law prohibiting discrimination against student groups based on religious, political, or philosophical grounds.

equal protection   The equal protection clause of the Fourteenth Amendment of the Constitution provides that "no state shall … deny to any person within its jurisdiction the equal protection of the laws." The equal protection clause has been interpreted by the U.S. Supreme Court to apply the entire Bill of Rights to the states. This requires that the First Amendment's establishment clause and free exercise of religion clause apply to state and local governments.

established church   An established church is—in effect—an "official" church that is government-endorsed. The Anglican church in England is one example. When there is an established church there is no clear-cut line between the secular and the religious. In the United States, six of the original thirteen colonies—Connecticut, Georgia, Maryland, Massachusetts, New Hampshire, and South Carolina, had established churches. In these colonies the government used tax revenues to give direct financial support to the established church. Although the established church was government-endorsed, each of these colonies also allowed a certain amount of toleration for other sects. The establishment clause of the First Amendment, which provides that the federal government shall make no laws "respecting the establishment of religion," prohibits the federal government from creating an established church.

establishment clause   The establishment clause of the First Amendment provides that the federal government shall make no laws "respecting the establishment of religion." The courts have held that it also applies to state and local governments. Over the years the language has been understood not only to prohibit the federal government from sponsoring a church but also against enacting laws that favor one church over another. For example, the clause has been interpreted to prohibit government support for religious schools, including the payment of salaries of teachers in religious schools even though they teach nonreligious subjects. Some have suggested that while the free exercise clause guarantees "freedom of religion," the establishment clause guarantees "freedom from religion."

evangelical　An evangelical Christian is one who has an intense personal relationship with Jesus. Evangelical Christians typically have a "born again" experience in which they have an emotional, personal experience with Jesus that reignites their religious experience. Spreading the word of God through evangelism is an important aspect of this movement. There is no specific religion or group by this name; the term is applied to particular individuals or churches. Evangelicals typically are conservative Christians who may believe in the literal truth of biblical scripture and that Christian values and beliefs need to be extended not only to other individuals but also to institutions like the public schools.

evidence　Information presented in testimony or in documents that is used to persuade the fact finder (judge or jury) to decide the case for one side or the other.

evolution　Scientific theory that all life including plants, animals, and humans, has evolved from simpler organisms. In contrast to the biblical depiction of creation in Genesis, the theory proposes that life on earth began as a protoplasmic mass from which life forms evolved, becoming increasingly more complex over time. The origins of the theory can be traced to the Frenchman Jean Lamark as early as 1801. Evolution theory gained credibility by the mid 1800s based on the works of both Alfred Russel Wallace and Charles Darwin who independently focused on the operation of natural selection in evolution. In his *Origin of the Species,* Darwin posited that natural selection, based on adaptability, determined the ultimate success and survival of both individual organisms and species. Species evolve and originate as individual adaptive traits are passed on to offspring. Modern evolutionary theory is bolstered by the study of genetics and DNA, which provides scientific verification of the observations of Darwin and others. Evolution is disputed by "creationists," who believe that life on earth was created by God as literally depicted in the Bible's book of Genesis.

Fourteenth Amendment to the U.S. Constitution　Of the three post–Civil War Amendments (Thirteen, Fourteen, and Fifteen), the Fourteenth ultimately loomed largest. The Thirteenth Amendment abolished slavery, the Fifteenth gave the right to vote regardless of race or "previous condition of servitude." The Fourteenth Amendment provides a number of protections: "No state shall make or enforce any law which shall abridge the privileges and immunities of citizens of the United States; nor shall any State deprive any person of life, liberty or property, without due process of law; nor deny to any person within its jurisdiction the equal protection of these laws."

free exercise clause   The First Amendment of the U.S. Constitution prohibits the federal government from making any law "prohibiting the free exercise" of religion. Although the free exercise clause originally applied only to the federal government, the courts have held that it also applies to states and local governments. Since public schools are a part of the government their actions are judged under this clause.

fundamentalism   Conservative Christianity. The term was first used to describe Christians who subscribed to "The Fundamentals, a Testimony to the Truth," a series of pamphlets distributed from 1910 to 1915 espousing religious conservatism and denouncing the theory of evolution. Today the term generally has a pejorative meaning. These believers prefer to be referred to as evangelicals.

inerrancy   The belief that biblical scripture is absolutely and literally true. A person who accepts the absolute accuracy of scripture will regard scientific explanations that are at variance with scripture to be false. This includes explanations such as evolution and geological dating of the earth.

injunction   An order of the court prohibiting (or compelling) the performance of a specific act to prevent irreparable damage or injury.

judgment   The official decision of a court finally determining the respective rights and claims of the parties to a suit.

judicial review   In *Marbury v. Madison,* the U.S. Supreme Court arrogated to itself the right of judicial review—the right to determine if a law of Congress is constitutional. If the Court determines that a federal, state, or local law is contrary to the Constitution, then the law will be held invalid. For example, a statute allowing school prayer passed by a unanimous Congress would likely be held contrary to the establishment clause and held invalid.

jurisdiction   (1) The legal authority of a court to hear and decide a case. Concurrent jurisdiction exists when two courts have simultaneous responsibility for the same case; (2) the geographic area over which the court has authority to decide cases.

jurisprudence   The study of law and the structure of the legal system.

Lemon **test**   A test formulated by the U.S. Supreme Court in applying the establishment clause to actual cases. This three-part test was formulated in the Supreme Court case, *Lemon v. Kurtzman* (1971). This test is used to determine if a particular law is in violation of the First Amendment's guarantee that the state will not establish a religion. Although the *Lemon* case has not been overruled, the Supreme Court has been reluctant to use the test since 1994.

litigation A case, controversy, or lawsuit. Participants (plaintiffs and defendants) in lawsuits are called litigants.

magistrate judges Judicial officers who assist U.S. district judges in getting cases ready for trial and who may decide some criminal and civil trials when both parties agree to have the case heard by a magistrate judge instead of a judge.

moment of silence *See* silence.

Monkey trial The still-famous 1925 "monkey" trial in which a Tennessee biology teacher, John Thomas Scopes, challenged a state law forbidding the teaching of evolution in public schools. Scopes was represented by Clarence Darrow and the state by William Jennings Bryan. Although Scopes was found guilty of violating the law, most commentators felt the anticreationists gained the most from the case's high visibility. However, laws prohibiting the teaching of evolution persisted in Arkansas and Mississippi until the mid 1960s.

nativists Pre–Civil War political movement that was opposed to the presence of immigrants in the United States. Often the movement had a strong anti-Catholic flavor. The movement was characterized by secret societies whose members when asked to reveal the society's views would respond "I know nothing." The movement became a political party—the "Know Nothings"—and enjoyed considerable success in New York and Pennsylvania. The movement also hatched compulsory education laws aimed at Catholic schools.

opinion A judge's written explanation of a decision of the court or of a majority of judges. A dissenting opinion disagrees with the majority opinion because of the reasoning and/or the principles of law on which the decision is based. A concurring opinion agrees with the decision of the court but offers further comment.

oral argument An opportunity for lawyers to summarize their position before the court and also to answer the judge's questions.

original intent Intent of the drafters. Most legal scholars accept that the Constitution's language needs to be interpreted flexibly to enable the courts to deal with contemporary situations. For example, the drafters of the Constitution could not have envisioned the legal problems posed by the Internet. However, other scholars believe that constitutional provisions need to be interpreted as closely as possible according to the original intent of the drafters. This would typically give the provisions less scope. For example, although the courts currently ban school prayer based on the establishment clause, an analysis based on original intent might show that there is no evidence that the drafters desired such a result.

panel (1) In appellate cases, a group of judges (usually three) assigned to decide the case; (2) in the jury selection process, the group of potential jurors.

parties Plaintiffs and defendants (petitioners and respondents) to lawsuits, also known as appellants and appellees in appeals, and their lawyers.

plaintiff The person who files the complaint in a civil lawsuit.

pleadings Written statements of the parties in a civil case of their positions. In the federal courts, the principal pleadings are the complaint and the answer.

pledge of allegiance Patriotic pledge typically recited by students at the start of each school day. The words "under God" were not inserted until 1954.

postmillennialism Belief in the second coming of Jesus Christ after one thousand years of human progress.

precedent A court decision in an earlier case with facts and law similar to a dispute currently before a court. Precedent will ordinarily govern the decision of a later similar case, unless a party can show that it was wrongly decided or that it differed in some significant way.

premillennialism Belief in the second coming of Jesus Christ after a period of tribulation on Earth. Jesus will usher in a thousand-year reign on Earth for the righteous.

record A written account of all the acts and proceedings in a lawsuit.

release time/dismissed time A program in which a public school dismisses students early to attend religion classes away from the public school grounds, with parental permission. Typically classes will be offered at individual churches and children will attend the classes at the church at which they regularly worship. Release-time programs were upheld by the U.S. Supreme Court in *Zorach v. Clauson* (1952). Earlier release-time programs, in which religion classes were taught in public school classrooms during the release-time period, were struck down by the Supreme Court as a violation of the establishment clause in *Illinois ex. rel McCollum v. Board of Education* (1948).

Religious Freedom Restoration Act Federal law, passed in 1993 and declared unconstitutional by the Supreme Court in 1997, that provided, among other things, that federal, state, and local governments "shall not substantially burden a person's exercise of religion even if the burden results from a rule of general applicability . . . except that Government may substantially burden a person's exercise of religion if it demonstrates that application of the burden to the person (1) is in furtherance of a compelling government interest; and (2) is the least restrictive means of furthering that compelling interest." The act is intended to deal with the free exercise of religion, not to the establishment of religion by the government.

remand When an appellate court sends a case back to a lower court for further proceedings.

reverse An appellate court sets aside the decision of a lower court because of an error. A reversal is often followed by a remand.

salary supplement Amount paid to a parochial or other religious schoolteacher by the public schools for teaching nonreligious subjects. A few states sought to avoid the ban by providing "indirect" forms of support. Both Rhode Island and Pennsylvania experimented with supplementing the salaries of parochial schoolteachers on the theory that doing so would be less expensive than educating these students in the public school system. The practice was held to be unconstitutional by the Supreme Court in *Lemon v. Kurtzman* (1971). The Court ruled that the states were paying money to the parochial schools in violation of the establishment clause.

school prayer amendment Proposed amendment to the Constitution that would overturn the Supreme Court case *Engel v. Vitale* and its successors and would allow verbal, organized prayer in the public schools. Although the proposed amendment has gained ground on a number of occasions, including a strong endorsement by President Reagan, the amendment has never been enacted.

scientific creationism *See* creation science.

secular humanism A philosophical belief system that embraces human rationality, scientific knowledge, and an appreciation for the classics. Although similar to a religion, the emphasis is on the potentialities of humans without the help of God. Fundamentalist Christians attach the term "secular humanist" to individuals or institutions that try to exclude religion from the public schools or public life. Fundamentalists have attacked public school curriculums, labeling them humanistic, and saying that moral problems are approached without a discussion of God.

silence/moment of silence When organized verbal school prayers were outlawed by the Supreme Court, many school districts adopted a moment of silence in their place. Students were instructed by their teachers to either pray or meditate before they started their class routines. The Supreme Court struck down one such law in *Wallace v. Jaffree* (1985), reasoning that, although children could be excused from the classroom, the moment of silence was a disguised compulsory school prayer. Currently, a moment of silence may be acceptable if the law creating it does not disguise prayer.

statute A law passed by a legislature.

statute of limitations A law that sets the time within which parties must take action to enforce their rights.

summary judgment A decision made on the basis of statements and evidence presented for the record without a trial. It is used when there is no dispute as to the facts of the case, and one party is entitled to judgment as a matter of law.

temporary restraining order (TRO)   Prohibits a person from an action that is likely to cause irreparable harm. This differs from an injunction in that it may be granted immediately, without notice to the opposing party, and without a hearing. It is intended to last only until a hearing can be held.

testimony   Evidence presented orally by witnesses during trials or before grand juries.

textbook lending   Lending of nonreligious public school textbooks by the government to parochial schools. A few states sought to avoid the ban on aid to public schools by providing indirect forms of support, for example, supplying textbooks either directly to the parochial schools or to the students themselves. The rationale is that this form of subsidy is still less expensive for the taxpayer than educating the students in the public school system. A divided Supreme Court upheld the practice in *Board of Education v. Allen* (1968), reasoning that the aid went to the students or their parents rather than to the school. The Court has also approved reimbursement of the costs of state-mandated standardized tests but has disapproved of providing free teaching materials other than textbooks.

tuition reimbursement   Reimbursement by the government of school tuition at private and parochial schools. The Supreme Court has held that such reimbursement—whether direct or indirect through tax credits—is unconstitutional in *Committee v. Nyquist* (1973) and *Sloan v. Lemon* (1973). More recently a closely divided Court upheld a Minnesota plan that granted a tax deduction for private school tuition in *Mueller v. Allen* (1983).

verdict   The decision of a petit jury or a judge.

vouchers   A system that allows the parents of a school-age child to receive a state-paid voucher to be used to pay tuition in private or religious schools. The aid is clearly to the family, but the family can choose to use the voucher in a religious school. Although the city of Milwaukee currently has a voucher system, the constitutionality of vouchers is still an open question.

wall of separation   Phrase originally used by Thomas Jefferson to describe the proper relationship of religion and the federal government. The phrase was used in Jefferson's 1802 letter to the Connecticut Baptists Association of Danbury, which read, in part: "Believing with you that religion is a matter which lies solely between man and his God, that he owes account to none other for his faith or his worship, that the legislative powers of government reach actions only, and not opinions, I contemplate with sovereign reverence that act of the whole American people which declared that their legislature should "make no law respecting an establishment of religion, or prohibiting the free exercise thereof, thus building a wall of separation between church and state."

Index

J ames John Jurinski is associate professor of law at the University of Portland. He is a certified tax attorney and author of several books and articles on legal topics. He specializes in first amendment issues.